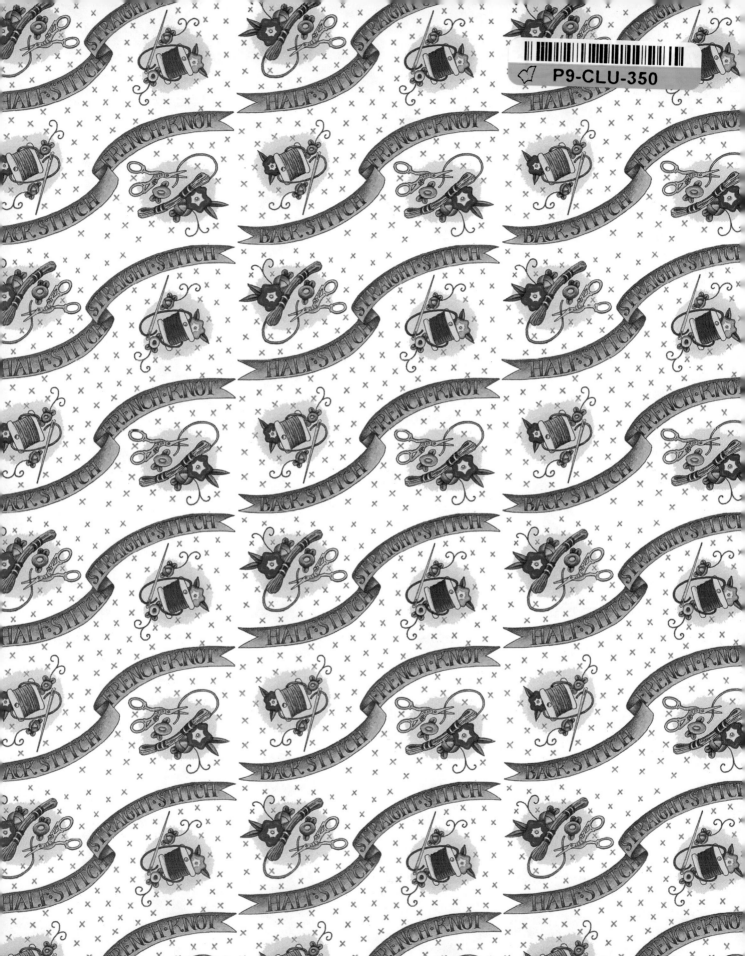

Meredith® Press
Des Moines, Iowa

Meredith® Press
An imprint of Meredith® Books

Mary Engelbreit Cross-Stitch
Editor: Christopher Cavanaugh
Contributing Editor and Writer: Sylvia Miller
Contributing Technical Editor: Susan Banker
Acquisition Editor: Maryanne Bannon
Contributing Art Director: Gayle Schadendorf
Copy Chief: Angela K. Renkoski
Photographers: Hopkins Associates and Scott Little
Technical Illustrator: Chris Neubauer Graphics
Photo Stylist and Project Designer: Margaret Sindelar
Project Coordinator: Dorinda Beaumont
Electronic Production Coordinator: Paula Forest
Production Manager: Douglas Johnston
Prepress Coordinator: Marjorie J. Schenkelberg

Meredith® Books
Editor in Chief: James D. Blume
Director, New Product Development: Ray Wolf

Vice President, Retail Marketing: Jamie L. Martin

Meredith Publishing Group
President, Publishing Group: Christopher Little
Vice President and Publishing Director: John P. Loughlin

Meredith Corporation
Chairman of the Board and Chief Executive Officer: Jack D. Rehm
President and Chief Operating Officer: William T. Kerr

Chairman of the Executive Committee: E. T. Meredith III

Cover Photograph: Hopkins Associates
Cover Illustration: Mary Engelbreit Studios

All of us at Meredith® Press are dedicated to providing you with the information and ideas you need to create beautiful and useful projects. We guarantee your satisfaction with this book for as long as you own it. We welcome your questions, comments, and suggestions. Please write to us at: Meredith® Press, Crafts, RW-240, 1716 Locust Street, Des Moines, IA 50309–3023.

Library of Congress Catalog Card Number: 96-76684
ISBN: 0-696-04665-2

GREETINGS

Mary Engelbreit's artwork captures life's special moments. Nearly 14 million of Mary's greeting cards help friends and families communicate their heartfelt feelings each year.

Now, for the first time, a book presents the talents of this popular artist in detailed charts so you can express your sentiments with cross-stitch artistry.

Each Mary Engelbreit note-card design is charted in complete format as well as in segments for quicker stitching of extraordinary projects.

Count on fun as you express yourself with these warm and lively cross-stitch messages.

CONTENTS

Artwork is appreciated by all, but I feel a special joy as I create my drawings. Now you can capture that fun with a needle and floss.

Any design worked in cross-stitch is an expression of love. Stitchery also speaks of patience as well as heartfelt appreciation of color and design. And, since so many cross-stitch projects are given as presents, I always think of friendship and family ties when I see a framed piece of fabric and floss.

It's fitting that my designs are now available on cross-stitch charts, because many of my original drawings were created for friends. Friendship is so important to me. It is by far the easiest subject for me to illustrate. One of my weaknesses is that I usually give my original drawings away—to friends. The Cross Country design on page 142 was a Christmas gift for a friend in Vermont who is a skier. Brotherly Love, shown on page 78, was given to dear friends with two boys who were moving to Colorado.

As with friendships, cross-stitch pieces are silent testament to permanence. Many are handed down in families through generations. As an artist, I draw inspiration from textiles, books, and illustrations that have survived the passing of time. If it's old, I love it! My house, studio, and designs are sweetened with time-honored treasures, so the thought that my designs will become family cross-stitch heirlooms is deeply pleasing to me.

My appreciation of the past includes vintage sayings and quotations. Many come from my secret treasure trove of women's and children's magazines from the 1920s and '30s. I find that words of wisdom, such as those in the Be Happy design on page 36, are timeless. It was more than 100 years ago that Abraham Lincoln said that people are about as happy as they make up their minds to be, and his observation rings true today.

I have made up my mind to be happy, and, yes, life for me is pretty much a chair of bowlies. My husband, Phil Delano, runs my business in St. Louis. I am so grateful that I convinced him to leave his job as a juvenile court officer, since I am more myself as an artist than a business manager. I don't want to get bogged down running a company when what I really want to do is draw pictures. We work together with a staff of about 30 good friends in a renovated church. We recognize that the physical environment of our business is unique, but we are pleased when people comment on the positive, fun-filled attitude we all share. It may be rare in the business world, but I think it's the way life should be.

Each of the 12 chapters of this book features one of my favorite greeting card designs. Greeting cards were how I started my career, and today it is humbling to realize how many of my cards are sold each year in addition to stationery, note cards, invitations, gift wrap, and gift bags. My beginning was much more modest. As a hopeful children's book illustrator, I traveled to New York City with a portfolio stuffed with drawings. A kind agent suggested

At home with cross-stitch, Mary Engelbreit enjoys the peaceful setting of her porch.

I show my work instead to a greeting card company. The card company actually bought six of my drawings on the spot for the magnificent price of $50 each, a vast improvement upon the 25 cents I used to receive for the colored pencil drawings I sold as a high schooler in St. Louis.

From childhood, I have been enchanted with illustrations. One of my earliest memories is studying the drawings in the books my mother and grandmother read to me. My first artwork was laboriously copying pictures from Raggedy Ann and Andy books. When I was 9, I begged my mother to set up a studio for me. To appease me, she squeezed an art table into a linen closet. It was 108 degrees in that closet, but I adored it.

People ask how much of me there is in my drawings, and I guess there is a lot. Events that I remember from childhood, such as filling a bird feeder, find their way onto my drawing paper. The bird feeder shown on page 126 was certainly influenced by that memory, although I know the structure was not as elaborate as I drew it.

Our sons, Evan, age 15, and Will, age 12, also influence my art. I drew the Nesting Place on page 110 thinking about Evan and how when he was little, he was so happy climbing trees. A favorite quotation of my mother's was the spark for Helping Hands on page 64. Mom was always right: Sweet remembrances do grow from good service.

Sometimes, I simply daydream and capture the results. The Sweet Home design on page 92 is one of those flights of fancy. I've always loved to draw cozy cottages flanked by flower beds, and I imagine myself living in that particular cottage.

I need daydreaming, too, to be able to conjure up the warmth and excitement of Christmas at any time, because Christmas is a year-round

Sun streams into Mary's studio at her home in St. Louis.

operation for everyone in our studio. The happy Santa on page 156 wears a coat of many colors, enlivened with (what else?) cherries. I firmly believe that since Santa needs to get dressed up only one night a year, he should wear the best outfit in the world. For some reason, I've always associated lions with Christmas. Maybe it's the lion-and-lamb parable. I remember starting on the drawing that is now Peace and Love on page 172 and having my first attempt be far more elaborate. The artwork here is my second, better, effort. It just goes to show you that sometimes it doesn't hurt to start over.

My designs are usually cheerful, but somber thoughts also bear fruit. I did the Comfort One Another artwork on page 50 when I was in a melancholy mood. The original quotation was much longer, but "Love comforteth like sunshine after rain" captures that feeling of needing a hug. I thought about making a book of similar thoughts, but after drawing three such works, I cured myself of the blues.

As you create cross-stitch versions of my designs, I'm confident you will create memories along with your finished artwork. As artists and crafters, we know the joy of watching a plain piece of paper or fabric come to life. When you are stitching and I am drawing, we can share the feeling that the roses are always in bloom, the cherries are always ripe, and good friends are always close at hand.

BEST WISHES

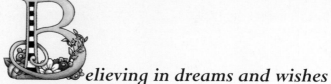

Believing in dreams and wishes come true, Mary Engelbreit shares the message with others in this best-selling note card artwork. Variations of the design lend charm to many accessories, including a birthday cake and girl's purse.

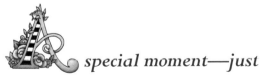

A special moment—just
before the penny is dropped—becomes a magical scene of hopes and
dreams. Stitch this framed piece, opposite, as a reminder of best wishes.

◦◦◦◦◦

*Present a birthday cake with its own greeting. A little frosting on this
collar, above, can be rinsed off for the next family birthday.*

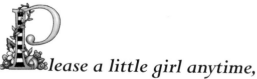

*P*lease *a little girl anytime,
but for a special gift, stitch this pretty pinafore, **above**. A necessary
accessory for any young lady, the matching bag with cross-stitch
embellishment makes a perfect keeping place for a stick of gum, a
penny or two, and other treasures.*

*Our pillow with its gold coin charms, **opposite**, offers family and guests a
penny for their thoughts.*

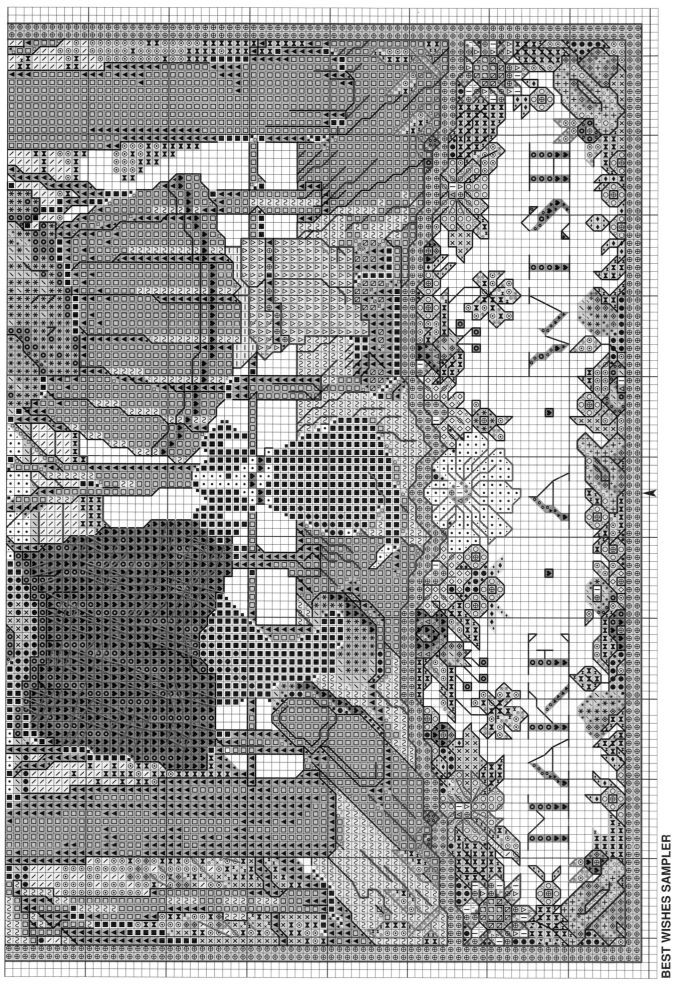

BEST WISHES SAMPLER

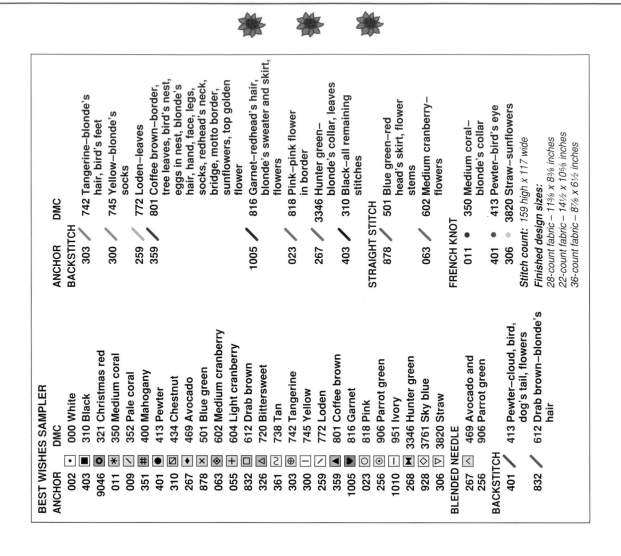

BEST WISHES SAMPLER

Dream a little while you stitch this scene where wishes are sure to come true (shown on page 10). Finished design is 11⅜×8⅜ inches.

MATERIALS

FABRIC
18×14-inch piece of 28-count ice blue Annabelle fabric

THREADS
Cotton embroidery floss in colors listed in the key above
Three additional skeins of white
One additional skein of DMC 310, 321, 350, 413, 434, 469, 612, 742, 816, 906, and 3346

SUPPLIES
Needle; embroidery hoop
Frame and mat of choice

INSTRUCTIONS

Tape or zigzag edges of fabric to prevent fraying. Find the center of the chart and the center of the fabric. Begin stitching there.

Work cross-stitches using three plies of floss over two threads of the Annabelle fabric. Use two plies of floss to work the backstitches, straight stitches, and French knots.

Press finished stitchery on wrong side with a warm iron.

Frame and mat as desired.

CAKE COLLAR

Celebrate birthdays with a special cake. This collar can be used time after time (shown on page 11). Stitched portion is 2⅛×8⅜ inches.

MATERIALS

FABRICS
3×30-inch piece of 14-count perforated plastic
3×30-inch piece of felted imitation suede fabric

THREADS
Cotton embroidery floss in colors listed in the key on page 17 plus one skein of DMC 828

SUPPLIES
Needle; crafts glue
½ yard of ½-inch-wide satin ribbon

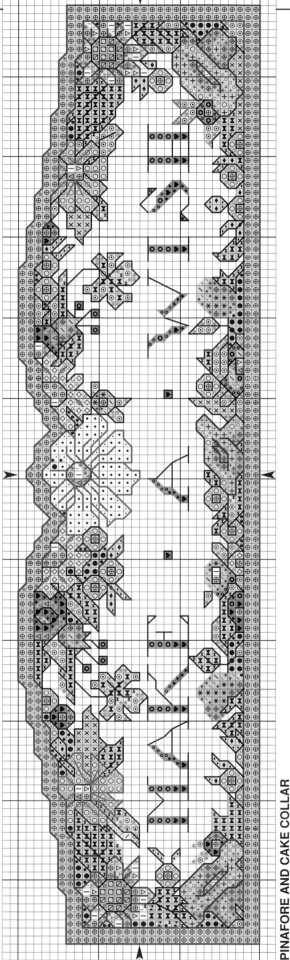

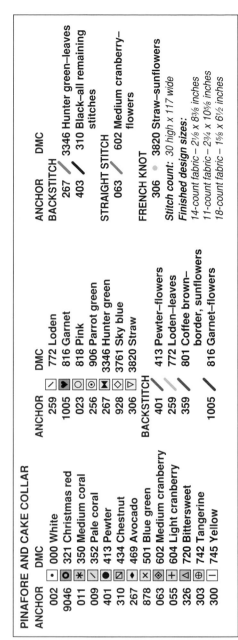

PINAFORE AND CAKE COLLAR

ANCHOR		DMC	
002	•	000	White
9046	◉	321	Christmas red
011	✳	350	Medium coral
009	◢	352	Pale coral
401	●	413	Pewter
310	◩	434	Chestnut
267	◆	469	Avocado
878	✕	501	Blue green
063	◈	602	Medium cranberry
055	◬	604	Light cranberry
326	⊕	720	Bittersweet
303	⊞	742	Tangerine
300	—	745	Yellow

ANCHOR		DMC	
259	╱	772	Loden
1005	◪	816	Garnet
023	◯	818	Pink
256	⊠	906	Parrot green
267	◈	3346	Hunter green
928	▷	3761	Sky blue
306	▷	3820	Straw

BACKSTITCH

401	╱	413	Pewter–flowers
259	╱	772	Loden–leaves
359	╱	801	Coffee brown– border, sunflowers
1005	╱	816	Garnet–flowers

ANCHOR		DMC	
267	╱	3346	Hunter green–leaves
403	╱	310	Black–all remaining stitches

STRAIGHT STITCH

063	╱	602	Medium cranberry– flowers

FRENCH KNOT

306	•	3820	Straw–sunflowers

Stitch count: 30 high x 117 wide

Finished design sizes:
14-count fabric – 2⅛ x 8⅜ inches
11-count fabric – 2¾ x 10⅝ inches
18-count fabric – 1⅝ x 6½ inches

INSTRUCTIONS

Find the center of the chart and the center of the perforated plastic. Begin stitching there.

Work cross-stitches using three plies of floss. Use two plies of floss to work the backstitches, straight stitches, and French knots. Use DMC 828 to fill background around lettering with cross-stitches.

Trim perforated plastic one square beyond stitching, leaving a 2×10-inch "tail" on each side.

CHARMING PILLOW

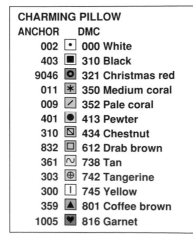

CHARMING PILLOW

ANCHOR		DMC		ANCHOR		DMC		ANCHOR		DMC
002	•	000 White		256	◉	906 Parrot green		**BACKSTITCH**		
403	■	310 Black		1010	–	951 Ivory		267	/	3346 Hunter green–
9046	◎	321 Christmas red		267	⋈	3346 Hunter green				girl's collar, leaves
011	✱	350 Medium coral		306	▽	3820 Straw		403	/	310 Black–all remaining
009	╱	352 Pale coral		**BACKSTITCH**						stitches
401	●	413 Pewter		832	/	612 Drab brown–girl's hair		**FRENCH KNOT**		
310	◪	434 Chestnut		303	/	742 Tangerine–girl's hair		1005	•	816 Garnet–girl's collar
832	▢	612 Drab brown		300	/	745 Yellow–girl's socks		*Stitch count:* 88 high x 64 wide		
361	∼	738 Tan		359	/	801 Coffee brown–girl's hair,		*Finished design sizes:*		
303	⊕	742 Tangerine				hand, face, legs, socks		*28-count fabric – 6¼ x 4⅝ inches*		
300	⎮	745 Yellow		1005	/	816 Garnet–girl's		*22-count fabric – 8 x 5⅞ inches*		
359	▲	801 Coffee brown				sweater and skirt		*36-count fabric – 4⅞ x 3½ inches*		
1005	♥	816 Garnet								

PENNY PURSE

ANCHOR		DMC	
403	◼	310	Black
9046	◉	321	Christmas red
011	✱	350	Medium coral
009	╱	352	Pale coral
401	●	413	Pewter
267	◆	469	Avocado
303	⊕	742	Tangerine
300	▯	745	Yellow
1005	♥	816	Garnet
306	▽	3820	Straw

BACKSTITCH

359	╱	801 Coffee brown–border, golden flower
403	╱	310 Black–all remaining stitches

Stitch count: 11 high x 94 wide
Finished design sizes:
28-count fabric – ¾ x 6¾ inches
22-count fabric – 1 x 8½ inches
36-count fabric – ⅝ x 5¼ inches

PENNY
PURSE
PATTERN

Place on fold

Cut suede fabric ⅛ inch larger than perforated plastic. Make a 2-inch slit in suede fabric on each side where stitching ends.

Place perforated plastic on top of suede; slip unstitched tails through slits behind the suede. Glue stitched portion in place.

Tack bows at edges of stitchery, if desired.

CHARMING PILLOW

A child, a penny, and a puppy are the simple pleasures on this pillow (shown on page 13).
Finished pillow is 14×12½ inches, including flange.

MATERIALS
FABRICS
14×12-inch piece of 28-count cream Annabelle fabric
¾ yard plaid corduroy
16×14-inch piece of fleece
⅓ yard white cotton fabric

THREADS
Cotton embroidery floss in colors listed in the key on page 18
SUPPLIES
Needle; embroidery hoop
Five ⅜-inch-diameter gold coin charms
7-inch zipper
1¾ yards of ¾-inch flat braid
Polyester fiberfill

INSTRUCTIONS
Tape or zigzag edges of Annabelle fabric to prevent fraying. Find the center of the chart and the center of the fabric. Begin stitching there.

Work cross-stitches using three plies of floss over two threads of Annabelle fabric. Use two plies to work the backstitches and French knots. Using photograph on page 13 as a guide, stitch charms in place.

Trim Annabelle fabric to 9×7½ inches with the stitched design centered.

Cut 2 corduroy strips 4×15 inches and 2 strips 4×13½ inches. To

make pillow front, with right sides together, stitch the corduroy strips to all sides of the Annabelle fabric, using a ½-inch seam allowance. Miter the four corners.

Place fleece on back of pillow front, basting along outside edge.

Cut one 12×13½-inch piece and one 4×13½-inch piece from corduroy for pillow back. Sew the two back pieces together, inserting zipper in center.

Place pillow back, with zipper open, on top of pillow front with right sides together and zipper at bottom edge. Stitch all sides, using ½-inch seam. Clip corners and turn.

Topstitch through all layers, 1 inch from Annabelle fabric and 2 inches from outer edge to make the flange.

Stitch flat braid to the outside edge of the pillow.

Cut cotton fabric into two 11×9½-inch pieces to make pillow form. Stitch together, using ½-inch seams, leaving an opening for turning. Turn and fill with polyester fiberfill. Whipstitch the opening closed. Insert pillow form inside pillow through zipper opening.

PINAFORE

Designed around your stitching, this pinafore can be made without a purchased pattern and will delight any young girl (shown on page 12). Finished bib is 3¼×9½ inches, including ½-inch ruffle.

MATERIALS
FABRICS
7×14-inch piece of 28-count ice blue Annabelle fabric
9×3-inch piece of fleece
1½ yards of main color cotton fabric
1¾ yards of contrasting fabric
THREADS
Cotton embroidery floss in colors listed in the key on page 17
SUPPLIES
Needle
Embroidery hoop
3 yards of ⅛-inch-diameter piping
Two ⅜-inch-diameter buttons

INSTRUCTIONS
Tape or zigzag edges of Annabelle fabric to prevent fraying. Find the center of the chart on page 17 and the center of the Annabelle fabric. Begin stitching there.

Work cross-stitches using three plies of floss over two threads of the Annabelle fabric. Use two plies of floss to work the backstitches, straight stitches, and French knots.

Trim Annabelle fabric, leaving ¾ inch below stitching across the bottom and ¾ inch on each side. Leave 1 inch above the center top of the stitching, curving slightly to ⅜ inch above stitching on each end.

Cut one piece of fleece and one piece of main color fabric the same size as Annabelle fabric. Also from main color fabric, cut two 3×18-inch strips for pinafore straps, two 2½×24-inch waistband pieces, and two 13×31-inch pieces for the skirt front and back. From contrasting fabric, cut a 2×24-inch bias strip for the bib ruffle and a 6×120-inch bias strip for the bottom ruffle (piecing strips as necessary).

Place fleece on wrong side of stitchery, basting around outside edge. Stitch a continuous piece of piping around top and two sides of cross-stitched bib front, using ½-inch seam allowance.

Fold the 2-inch bias strip lengthwise with wrong sides together; press along fold. Gather the raw-edge side, using ½-inch seam. Adjust gathers to fit sides and top of bib. Stitch on top of the piping.

Make straps by pressing ½-inch seam allowance to wrong sides of 3-inch strips. Fold lengthwise and press fold. Topstitch the length of each strap.

Stitch straps to front edges of bib, using photograph, *page 12,* as a guide. Stitch bib backing (cut from main color) to bib front with right sides together, leaving open across bottom edge.

Stitch bib centered between two waistband pieces. Join skirt front and back, gather to fit waistband, and stitch.

Stitch piping to lower edge of skirt. Join bias strip for bottom ruffle into a continuous circle. Fold lengthwise, wrong sides together, and press. Gather raw edges to fit bottom edge of skirt. Stitch on top of piping stitching line.

Finish waistband with two buttons and buttonholes at center back, making a small placket.

PENNY PURSE

Match the pinafore with the little drawstring purse (shown on page 12), or use the bag as a traveling case for jewelry or other items that get lost in a suitcase. Finished purse is 8½×6½ inches.

MATERIALS
FABRICS
4×10-inch piece of 28-count tan Jubilee cloth
⅓ yard of cotton fabric for bag
⅓ yard of cotton fabric for lining
THREADS
Cotton embroidery floss in colors listed in the key on page 19
SUPPLIES
Needle
Embroidery hoop
Tracing paper
1 yard of ⅛-inch-diameter piping
1 yard of ¼-inch-diameter cording for drawstring

INSTRUCTIONS
Tape or zigzag edges of fabric to prevent fraying. Find the center of the chart and the center of the fabric. Begin stitching there.

Work cross-stitches using three plies of floss over two threads of the Jubilee cloth. Use two plies of floss to work the backstitches.

Press finished stitchery on the wrong side with a warm iron.

Trace and complete oval pattern provided on page 19. Cut one bag bottom, using the oval pattern.

Cut two pieces for bag front: one 7½×7½-inch piece and one 2×7½-inch piece. Cut one 9½×7½-inch piece for bag back.

Cut bag lining by cutting one oval and two 9½×7½-inch pieces for front and back.

Trim Jubilee cloth to 2×7½ inches with stitching centered. Stitch cross-stitching between the top and bottom of the bag front, using ½-inch seam allowance. Stitch bag back to bag front, leaving a ½-inch opening in each side seam 2 inches from the top. Stitch side seams for lining.

Stitch piping to top edge of bag. With right sides together, stitch lining to bag around top edge, using the piping stitching line as a guide.

Stitch piping around bottom edge of bag. With bag wrong-side out, stitch oval bottom to bag. Stitch oval to bag lining, leaving an opening for turning.

Turn bag to right side and whipstitch opening in lining closed.

Make a casing by topstitching around bag 1½ inches from the top. Stitch again 2 inches from the top.

Cut cording in half. Thread one piece through the bag front casing and one through the back casing. Knot the ends. Gather the bag with the cording.

Breit Ideas

If wishes were stitches, making our dreams come true would be sew easy.

❋ Make stripes. Use the border chart for the Penny Purse as a stripe, repeating the chart to make desired length. Separate this stripe from the next with rows of solid cross-stitches. For added texture, select a coordinating color of linen and skip a few threads between rows. Reverse the direction (turn the fabric upside down) when you repeat a stripe of the charted border. Your creative stripes would make a great pillow top.

❋ A paper doll would be fun for the youngster you have taught to cross-stitch. Use the chart for the Charming Pillow to stitch the little girl on perforated paper. Take on the challenge of designing a different dress for changeable outfits for your paper doll.

❋ Puppy love can be stitched directly onto children's clothing. Use waste canvas to add this puppy to a back pocket on a pair of pants.

❋ The little bird on a fence post will make a cheerful greeting card. Stitch the post in entirety or cut it off with staggered stitches.

❋ Serve from a personalized tray. Use the flower-framed Best Wishes Sampler chart and substitute a family name or monogram for the words. Insert your stitching in a prefinished serving tray.

❋ Are you involved in a charity bazaar? A miniature wishing well can collect maximum contributions. Use the Best Wishes Sampler chart to stitch on perforated plastic to make an inviting label for your wishing well.

Flowers are lovely;
love is flower-like;
Friendship is a
sheltering tree.

Mary

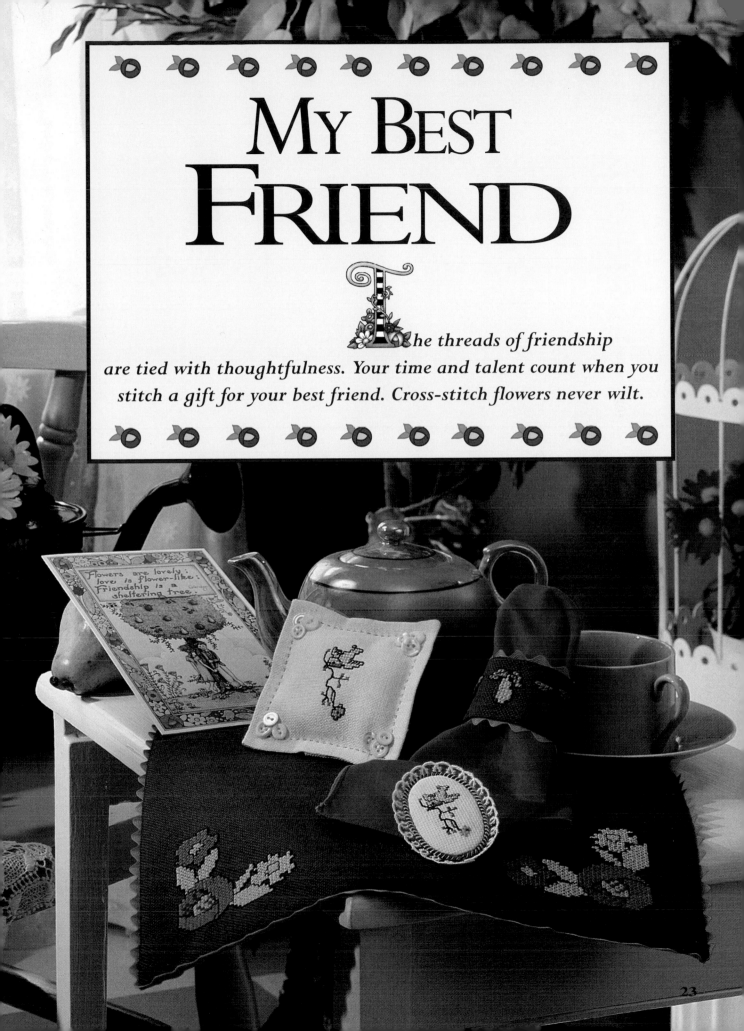

MY BEST FRIEND

*T*he threads of friendship are tied with thoughtfulness. Your time and talent count when you stitch a gift for your best friend. Cross-stitch flowers never wilt.

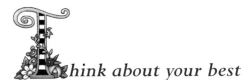

hink about your best friend as you thread your needle with the happy colors in this *Mary Engelbreit* design, left. Have fun stitching this lighthearted piece that features a tree bearing multiple varieties of fruit and flowers blooming everywhere.

Just a few stitches will send a happy message to a friend when you create this bluebird brooch or envelope sachet, above. These quick, easy gifts demonstrate how elements of the larger design can be used effectively—a perfect solution when you're short on time but not on caring.

 weet scents, packaged in little
handmade satchels, **above**, make special gifts. Or, treat yourself and tuck one
in your own dresser drawer. The flowers are charted for you, but you may
find additional elements from Mary Engelbreit's friendship design to
keep your creativity blooming.

A table set for your best friends, **opposite**, shows how much you care. Mary
Engelbreit's signature flowers (from the border of the friendship design)
appear on place mats and place cards. Colorful fruit from the
sheltering tree is stitched on a napkin ring.

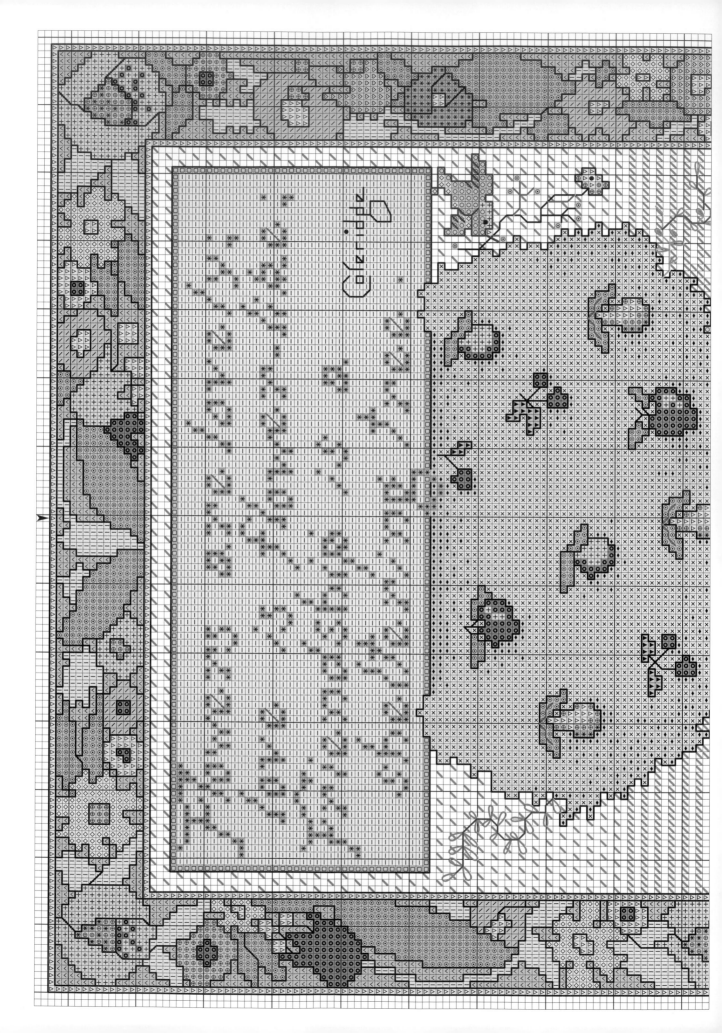

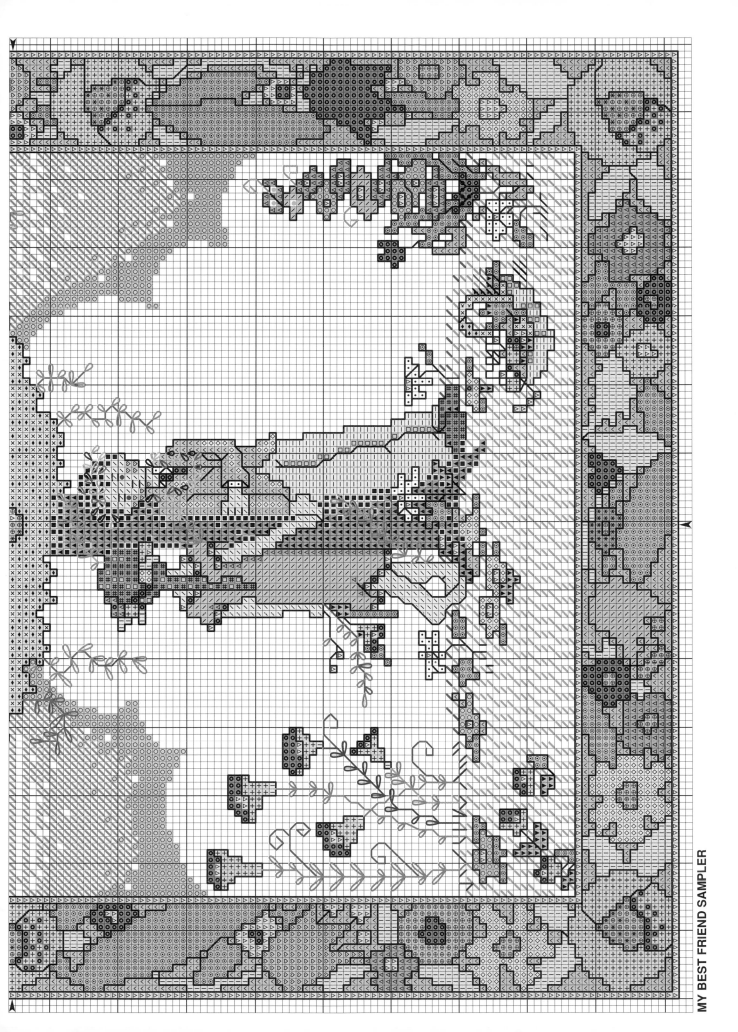

MY BEST FRIEND SAMPLER

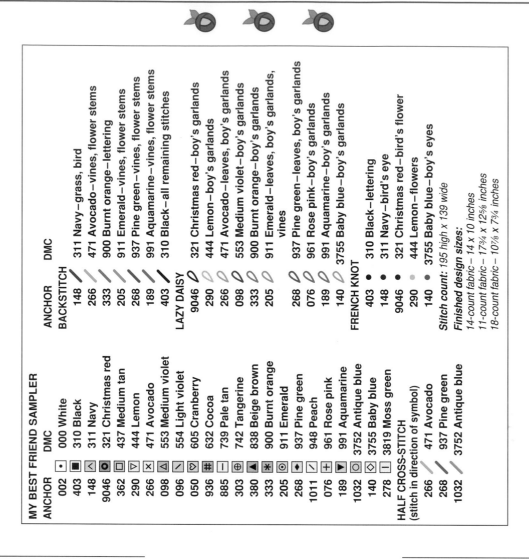

MY BEST FRIEND SAMPLER

ANCHOR	DMC		
002	000	•	White
403	310	■	Black
148	311	<	Navy
9046	321	⊙	Christmas red
362	437	□	Medium tan
290	444	▷	Lemon
266	471	×	Avocado
098	553	◁	Medium violet
096	554	/	Light violet
050	605	▷	Cranberry
936	632	#	Cocoa
885	739			Pale tan
303	742	⊕	Tangerine
380	838	◀	Beige brown
333	900	*	Burnt orange
205	911	⊙	Emerald
268	937	◆	Pine green
1011	948	◊	Peach
076	961	+	Rose pink
189	991	▶	Aquamarine
1032	3752	○	Antique blue
140	3755	◇	Baby blue
278	3819	—	Moss green

HALF CROSS-STITCH (stitch in direction of symbol)

ANCHOR	DMC		
266	471		Avocado
268	937		Pine green
1032	3752		Antique blue

BACKSTITCH

ANCHOR	DMC	
148	311	Navy–grass, bird
266	471	Avocado–vines, flower stems
333	900	Burnt orange–lettering
205	911	Emerald–vines, flower stems
268	937	Pine green–vines, flower stems
189	991	Aquamarine–vines, flower stems
403	310	Black–all remaining stitches

LAZY DAISY

ANCHOR	DMC	
9046	321	Christmas red–boy's garlands
290	444	Lemon–boy's garlands
266	471	Avocado–leaves, boy's garlands
098	553	Medium violet–boy's garlands
333	900	Burnt orange–boy's garlands
205	911	Emerald–leaves, boy's garlands, vines
268	937	Pine green–leaves, boy's garlands
076	961	Rose pink–boy's garlands
189	991	Aquamarine–boy's garlands
140	3755	Baby blue–boy's garlands

FRENCH KNOT

ANCHOR	DMC	
403	310	Black–lettering
148	311	Navy–bird's eye
9046	321	Christmas red–bird's flower
290	444	Lemon–flowers
140	3755	Baby blue–boy's eyes

Stitch count: 195 high x 139 wide
Finished design sizes:
14-count fabric – 14 x 10 inches
11-count fabric – 17¾ x 12⅝ inches
18-count fabric – 10⅞ x 7¾ inches

MY BEST FRIEND SAMPLER

This Mary Engelbreit friendship design (shown on page 24) *becomes a big-as-life message to be enjoyed every day of the year.*
Finished design is 14×10 inches.

MATERIALS
FABRIC
22×18-inch piece of 14-count white Aida cloth
THREADS
Cotton embroidery floss in colors listed in the key above
Three additional skeins of DMC 310
Two additional skeins of DMC 471 and 739
One additional skein of DMC 444, 911, 961, and 3752
SUPPLIES
Needle; embroidery hoop
Frame and mat of choice

INSTRUCTIONS
Tape or zigzag edges of fabric to prevent fraying. Find the center of the chart and the center of the fabric. Begin stitching there.

Work cross-stitches using three plies of floss. Note the special effect created by use of half cross-stitches in the sky area. Use two plies of floss to work the backstitches, lazy daisy stitches, and French knots.

Press finished stitchery on wrong side with a warm iron.

Frame and mat as desired.

PILLOW SACHET

This button-trimmed, fragrant, little pillow is a sweet symbol of friendship (shown on page 26). Finished sachet is 4×4 inches.

MATERIALS
FABRIC
7×12-inch piece of 28-count pastel beige linen
THREADS
Cotton embroidery floss in colors listed in the key on page 31
SUPPLIES
Needle; embroidery hoop
12 tiny buttons
Potpourri or other scented material to fill sachet

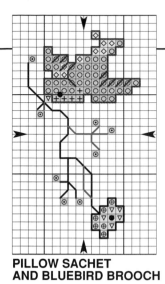

**PILLOW SACHET
AND BLUEBIRD BROOCH**

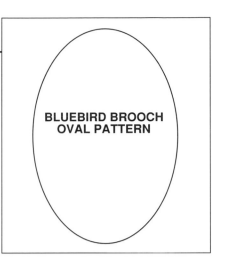

**PILLOW SACHET AND
BLUEBIRD BROOCH**

ANCHOR		DMC	
290	▽	444	Lemon
303	⊕	742	Tangerine
205	⊙	911	Emerald
076	+	961	Rose pink
1032	◯	3752	Antique blue
140	◇	3755	Baby blue

BACKSTITCH

148	/	311	Navy – bird
189	/	991	Aquamarine – vines
403	/	310	Black – all remaining stitches

FRENCH KNOT

9046	●	321	Christmas red – flower
140	●	3755	Baby blue – bird's eye

Stitch count: 26 high x 14 wide
Finished design sizes:
18-count fabric – 1⅜ x ¾ inches
14-count fabric – 1⅞ x 1 inches
11-count fabric – 2⅜ x 1¼ inches

INSTRUCTIONS

Tape or zigzag edges of linen to prevent fraying. Find the center of the chart and the center of the fabric. Begin stitching there.

Work cross-stitches using three plies of floss over two threads of the linen. Use two plies of floss to work the backstitches and French knots.

Trim linen to a 5×10-inch piece, trimming 1 inch from each side.

Stitch ½-inch hem in both short ends of fabric. Fold fabric with right sides together into thirds (center of embroidery should be 2 inches from each fold). Hemmed edges will

overlap on back of sachet. Stitch across raw edges, making ½-inch seams through all layers. Trim seams, turn right side out; press flat.

Use three plies of DMC 3755 floss to work a row of running stitches through all layers, ⅜ inch from the edges on all four sides of the sachet.

Tack three buttons in each corner.

BLUEBIRD BROOCH

Pin a bluebird of happiness (shown on page 25) on your shoulder.
Finished brooch is 2¼×1½ inches.

MATERIALS
FABRICS
6×6-inch piece of 18-count white Aida cloth
4×4-inch piece of felt
6×6-inch piece of fleece
THREADS
Cotton embroidery floss in colors listed in the key above left
SUPPLIES
Needle; embroidery hoop
Tracing paper
3×2-inch piece of cardboard
3×3-inch piece of paper-backed iron-on adhesive
Crafts glue
¼ yard of ⅛-inch-diameter blue cord
¼ yard of ¼-inch-wide white lace
1-inch-long pin back

INSTRUCTIONS

Tape or zigzag edges of fabric to prevent fraying. Find center of chart and center of Aida cloth. Begin stitching there.

Work cross-stitches using two plies of floss. Use one ply of floss to work backstitches and two plies to work French knots.

Press finished stitchery on wrong side with a warm iron.

**BLUEBIRD BROOCH
OVAL PATTERN**

Trace and cut out oval pattern. Cut oval from one piece of cardboard, one piece of paper-backed adhesive, one piece of felt, and two pieces of fleece.

Glue one piece of fleece to the cardboard oval.

Fuse paper-backed adhesive to remaining fleece oval. Remove paper and center the stitched design on fleece; fuse fleece to back of stitchery.

Place two pieces of fleece together and trim cross-stitched fabric ½ inch larger than cardboard backing. Clip ¼-inch notches at ½-inch intervals around edge. Glue clipped edge to cardboard back.

Cut blue cord to fit outer edge. Glue in place, trimming and butting ends. Glue lace behind cording.

Glue oval piece of felt to back. Glue pin back to center of the felt.

DRAWSTRING SACHET

Ribbon bows accent your stitchery in this easy-to-make bag (shown on page 26).
Finished bag is 5½×2½ inches.

MATERIALS
FABRICS
5¾×13-inch piece of 28-count light pastel blue linen
3¾×11-inch piece of fabric of choice for lining
THREADS
Cotton embroidery floss in colors listed in the key on page 32

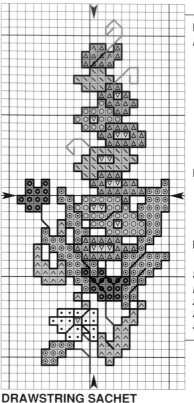

DRAWSTRING SACHET

DRAWSTRING SACHET			
ANCHOR		DMC	
002	•	000	White
148	△	311	Navy
9046	◉	321	Christmas red
290	▽	444	Lemon
098	◮	553	Medium violet
096	◣	554	Light violet
205	◉	911	Emerald
1032	◯	3752	Antique blue
BACKSTITCH			
148	╱	311	Navy–flower stems
266	╱	471	Avocado–vines
403	╱	310	Black–all remaining stitches
FRENCH KNOT			
290	•	444	Lemon–flowers

Stitch count: 44 high x 19 wide
Finished design sizes:
28-count fabric – 3⅛ x 1⅜ inches
22-count fabric – 4 x 1¾ inches
36-count fabric – 2⅜ x 1 inches

SUPPLIES
Needle; embroidery hoop
1 yard of ⅜-inch-wide satin ribbon
Potpourri or other scented material

INSTRUCTIONS
Tape or zigzag edges of linen to prevent fraying. Fold the linen in half and mark the center of one half (fold is the bottom, raw edge the top). Unfold. Find the center of the chart and begin stitching there.

Work cross-stitches using three plies of floss over two threads of the linen. Use two plies of floss to work the backstitches and French knots.

Press finished stitchery on wrong side with a warm iron.

Trim linen to 3¾×11 inches (trimming 1 inch from each side). Place lining fabric on top of stitchery with right sides together. Using a ½-inch seam allowance, stitch across one short end and down ½ inch on side. Leave ½ inch open, and stitch another ½ inch. Repeat on other side. Repeat on other short end. Clip corners. Turn right side out and press.

Topstitch two rows across the short end (½ inch from top and 1 inch from top), forming a casing. Repeat at other end.

Stitch sides of the linen bag and sides of lining. Tuck lining inside linen bag.

Cut ribbon in half. Thread one piece through the casing on one side of the bag; repeat for other side. Fill bag loosely with potpourri or other scented material. Gather top of bag with ribbon, tie bows, and trim ends.

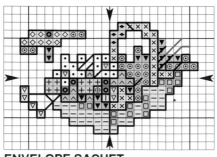

ENVELOPE SACHET

ENVELOPE SACHET
This button-closed packet of sweet scent (shown on page 25) also could be used as a jewelry case or treasure keeper. The two motifs, selected from the friendship design and charted here, give you a choice in decorating your sachet—or you may decide to stitch them both. Finished sachet is 3½×5¼ inches.

MATERIALS
FABRICS
10×15-inch piece of 28-count pastel pink linen
6×8-inch piece of fabric of choice for lining
THREADS
Cotton embroidery floss in colors listed in key below or on page 33
SUPPLIES
Needle; embroidery hoop
⅓ yard of ¼-inch-wide lace
⅜-inch button
Potpourri or other scented material

ENVELOPE SACHET			
ANCHOR		DMC	
002	•	000	White
148	△	311	Navy
9046	◉	321	Christmas red
362	▢	437	Medium tan
290	▽	444	Lemon
266	✕	471	Avocado
885	▭	739	Pale tan
303	⊕	742	Tangerine
205	◉	911	Emerald
268	◆	937	Pine green
076	✚	961	Rose pink
189	▼	991	Aquamarine
140	◇	3755	Baby blue
278	▯	3819	Moss green
BACKSTITCH			
189	╱	991	Aquamarine–vines
403	╱	310	Black–all remaining stitches

Stitch count: 14 high x 22 wide
Finished design sizes:
28-count fabric – 1 x 1½ inches
22-count fabric – 1¼ x 2 inches
36-count fabric – ¾ x 1¼ inches

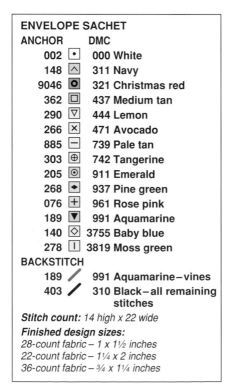

ENVELOPE SACHET

ANCHOR		DMC	
9046	◉	321	Christmas red
290	▽	444	Lemon
076	✛	961	Rose pink
278	Ⅰ	3819	Moss green

BACKSTITCH

403	╱	310	Black—flowers
205	╱	911	Emerald—vines, flower stems
189	╱	991	Aquamarine—vines

LAZY DAISY

205	⬭	911	Emerald—leaves

Stitch count: 14 high x 22 wide

Finished design sizes:
28-count fabric – 1 x 1½ inches
22-count fabric – 1¼ x 2 inches
36-count fabric – ¾ x 1¼ inches

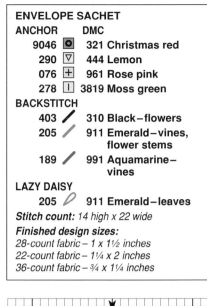

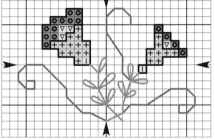

ENVELOPE SACHET

INSTRUCTIONS

Tape or zigzag edges of linen to prevent fraying. Find the center of the chart and the center of one 10-inch end of the linen. Measure 3 inches above the edge of the linen and match bottom center of chart to this spot. Begin stitching there.

Work cross-stitches using three plies of floss over two threads of the linen. Use two plies of floss to work the backstitches and lazy daisy stitches.

Press finished stitchery on wrong side with a warm iron.

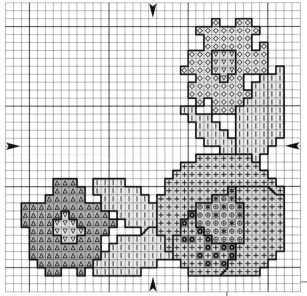

PLACE MAT

Trim fabric to 6×11 inches, cutting 2 inches from all four sides.

Fold the fabric in half lengthwise with right sides together. Stitch across the short end that is embroidered, making a ½-inch seam. Turn to right side and press to form the pointed flap. Turn under and press ½-inch seam allowance on back of pointed flap and on opposite side (short end) of fabric. Fold the fabric in half with right sides together, and stitch side seams using ½-inch seams; turn.

Press under ½-inch seam allowance on the two short ends of the lining fabric. Fold lining in half with right sides together (making a 4×5-inch rectangle). Stitch the 4-inch sides, using a ½-inch seam allowance.

Slip lining inside embroidered envelope; whipstitch in place. Whipstitch a piece of lace around the pointed flap.

Make a thread loop at the point of the flap. Sew button to front of the sachet to correspond with loop.

Fill bag loosely with potpourri or other scented material.

PLACE MAT

ANCHOR		DMC	
9046	◉	321	Christmas red
290	▽	444	Lemon
098	△	553	Medium violet
303	⊕	742	Tangerine
333	✳	900	Burnt orange
076	✛	961	Rose pink
140	◇	3755	Baby blue
278	Ⅰ	3819	Moss green

BACKSTITCH

403	╱	310	Black—all stitches

Stitch count: 32 high x 33 wide

Finished design sizes:
22-count fabric – 2⅞ x 3 inches
28-count fabric – 2¼ x 2¼ inches
36-count fabric – 1¾ x 1⅞ inches

PLACE MAT

Your table will blossom with Mary Engelbreit signature flowers at each setting (shown on page 27). Finished place mat is 12×18 inches.

MATERIALS

FABRICS

13×19-inch piece of 22-count Victorian Christmas green Hardanger fabric

13×19-inch piece of fleece for inner lining

13×19-inch piece of fabric of choice for backing

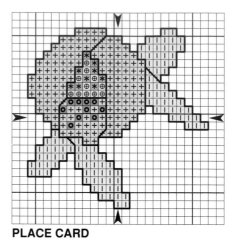

PLACE CARD

THREADS
Cotton embroidery floss in colors
listed in the key on page 33
SUPPLIES
Needle; embroidery hoop
1¾ yards of ½-inch-wide pink rickrack

INSTRUCTIONS

Zigzag edges of Hardanger fabric to prevent fraying. Measure 1½ inches from each edge. Mark the spot on each corner where the 1½-inch lines intersect. Find center of chart and begin stitching at center spot of one corner.

Work cross-stitches using three plies of floss over two threads of the Hardanger fabric. Use two plies of floss to work the backstitches. Rotate the chart 90 degrees to stitch the next corner. Repeat to stitch the third and fourth corners.

Press finished stitchery on wrong side with a warm iron.

Baste fleece to back side of cross-stitched Hardanger fabric, stitching along the outside edges of the fabric.

Stitch rickrack on the right side of the place mat, ½ inch from each edge, stitching in the center of the pink rickrack.

Place backing fabric on top of place mat with right sides together. Stitch on top of the rickrack stitching line, leaving an opening for turning. Trim seams, clip corners, and turn.

Whipstitch the opening closed.

PLACE CARD

Invite your guests to take home their place cards (shown on page 27) and use their cross-stitched flower on other items.
Flower motif is 2 inches in diameter.

MATERIALS
FABRIC
5×5-inch piece of 22-count ecru
Hardanger fabric*
THREADS
Cotton embroidery floss in colors
listed in the key at right
SUPPLIES
Needle
Water-based sealer for needlework
finishing
Double-sided tape
Place card of choice
*Optional fabrics: Aida Plus cloth or perforated paper (available only in 14-count). These fabrics will make a smaller design, but they eliminate the need to treat the edges before cutting out the design.

INSTRUCTIONS

Tape or zigzag edges of Hardanger fabric to prevent fraying. Find center of chart and fabric to begin stitching.

Work cross-stitches using three plies of floss over two threads of the Hardanger fabric. Use two plies for the backstitches.

Treat edges of design area with needlework sealer, following manufacturer's directions.

Cut out design carefully. Attach to a place card with double-sided tape.

PLACE CARD

PLACE CARD		
ANCHOR		DMC
9046	⊙	321 Christmas red
303	⊕	742 Tangerine
333	✳	900 Burnt orange
076	✚	961 Rose pink
278	☐	3819 Moss green
BACKSTITCH		
403	╱	310 Black–all stitches

Stitch count: 23 high x 23 wide
Finished design sizes:
22-count fabric – 2 x 2 inches
28-count fabric – 1⅝ x 1⅝ inches
36-count fabric – 1¼ x 1¼ inches

NAPKIN RING		
ANCHOR		DMC
9046	⊙	321 Christmas red
290	▽	444 Lemon
303	⊕	742 Tangerine
333	✳	900 Burnt orange
205	⊙	911 Emerald
076	✚	961 Rose pink
189	▼	991 Aquamarine
BACKSTITCH		
403	╱	310 Black–all stitches

Stitch count: 9 high x 37 wide
Finished design sizes:
22-count fabric – ⅞ x 3⅜ inches
28-count fabric – ⅝ x 2⅝ inches
36-count fabric – ½ x 2⅛ inches

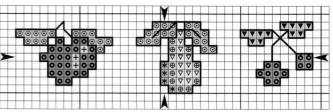

NAPKIN RING

NAPKIN RING

A perfect complement to your place mat, this napkin ring with its fresh-fruit trim (shown on page 27) *also can be used with other table linens. Finished size is 1½×6 inches.*

MATERIALS
FABRICS
2½×7-inch piece of 22-count Victorian Christmas green Hardanger fabric
2½×7-inch piece of fabric of choice for lining
THREADS
Cotton embroidery floss in colors listed in the key on page 34
SUPPLIES
½ yard of ½-inch-wide pink rickrack

INSTRUCTIONS
Zigzag edges of Hardanger fabric to prevent fraying. Find the center of the chart and the center of the fabric. Begin stitching there.

Work cross-stitches using three plies of floss over two threads of the Hardanger fabric. Use two plies of floss for backstitches.

Press finished stitchery on wrong side with a warm iron.

Stitch rickrack across each long side of fabric, ½ inch from edge, stitching in the center of the rickrack.

Place lining fabric on top of cross-stitched fabric with right sides together. Stitch ½-inch seams on both long sides, stitching on top of the rickrack stitching line. Turn tube to right side.

Tuck ½-inch seam allowances to the inside of each end of the tube.

Whipstitch the tube into a ring.

Breit Ideas

Opportunity, like a good friend, is knocking at your door with this friendship design.

🌀 The flower border can frame a photograph or a mirror for a special place in your home.

🌀 Trim a young girl's dress or pinafore with the flower border. If stitching enough for an entire skirt is overwhelming, just stitch a band for a pocket or trim the bib of an apron or pinafore.

🌀 Select flowers to stitch on cross-stitch bands. These evenweave fabrics with finished edges make everything from bookmarks to curtain tiebacks easy projects.

🌀 Add drama to your window. Use the border to edge a valance. Make it big and bold (and quick) by using 6-count fabric.

🌀 Love the "flowers are lovely" verse? Stitch just that portion, bringing the bottom border up to meet the lower edge of the message area.

🌀 Brighten your guest bath by stitching the border on a prefinished hand towel. Then use the flower (from the place mat) on a hand mirror. Use the same flower on a sachet bag or pillow. You can extend your room decor by inserting your stitchery into small ready-made trays and boxes. These border flowers are stitched in one main color, making it easy to substitute floss for a perfect match with your color scheme.

🌀 Baby gifts can be accented with your stitchery of this design. Use the sachet charts to decorate a baby bib or any of the many prefinished infant items available.

🌀 Send happy thoughts to your best friend by stitching a bluebird on a greeting card.

MOST FOLKS ARE ABOUT
AS HAPPY AS THEY MAKE
UP THEIR MINDS TO BE.
ABRAHAM LINCOLN

BE HAPPY

A smile will sneak up on your face every time you turn your attention to this heartwarming stitchery. Stitch the entire design or just one flowerpot, and spread good cheer to everyone.

Border a photo from a perfect summer day with this soft mat of hollyhocks, bees, and butterflies, above. Oranges cling to the branches of the tree and remind you of sweet fragrances. The hand mirror, above right, makes an elegant showcase for your cross-stitches.

The nostalgic art and friendly message of this framed piece, opposite, lighten a stress-filled day.

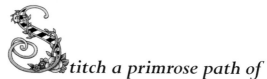
titch a primrose path of
flowerpots around a table mat, **above**, for the centerpiece of a happy table.
You'll find dozens of uses for this flowery clay-pot motif.

Smiling on one side, above, pouting on the other, left, this topsy-turvy doll will bring laughter wherever she goes. Just 7½ inches tall, she fits little hands perfectly.

41

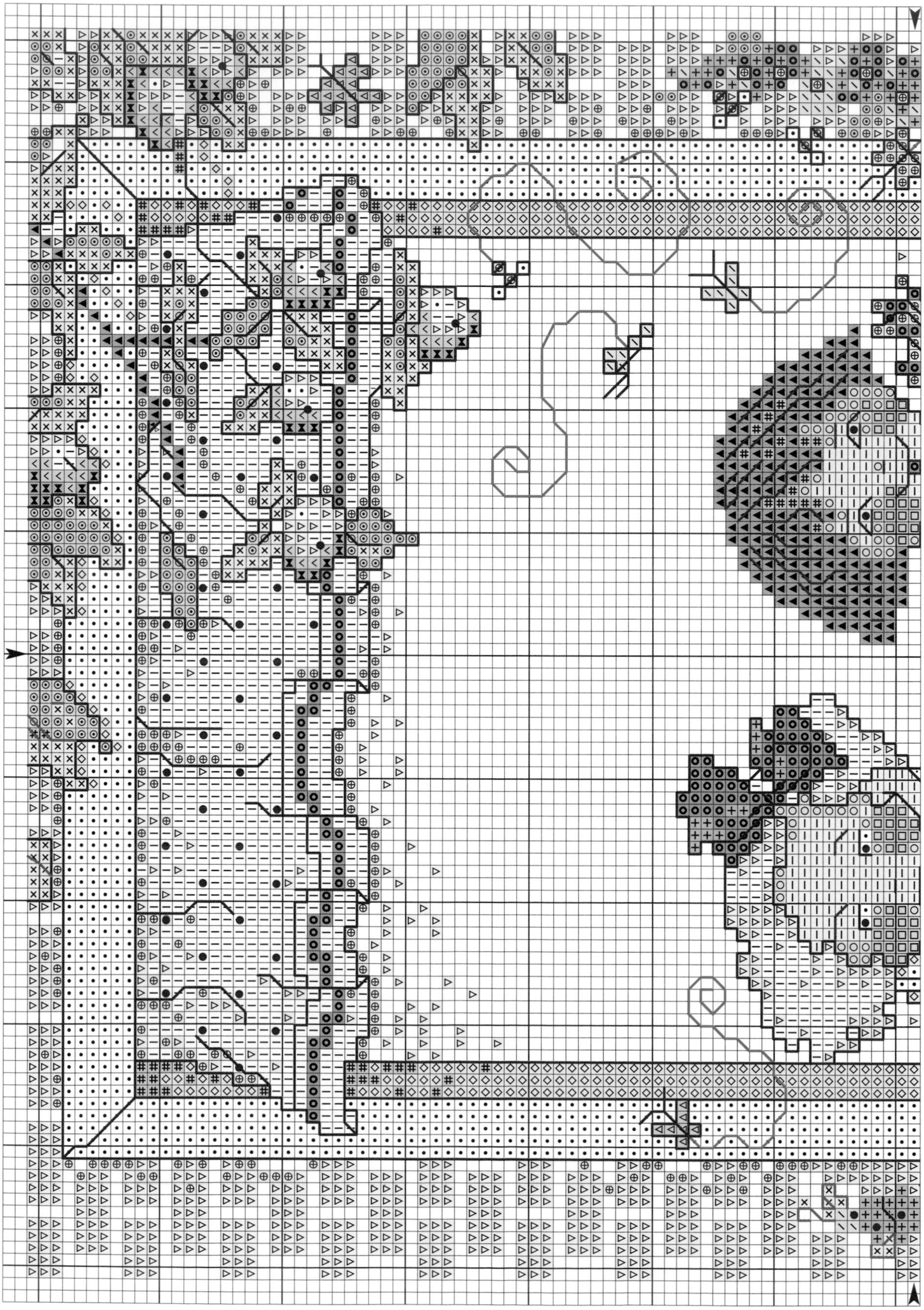

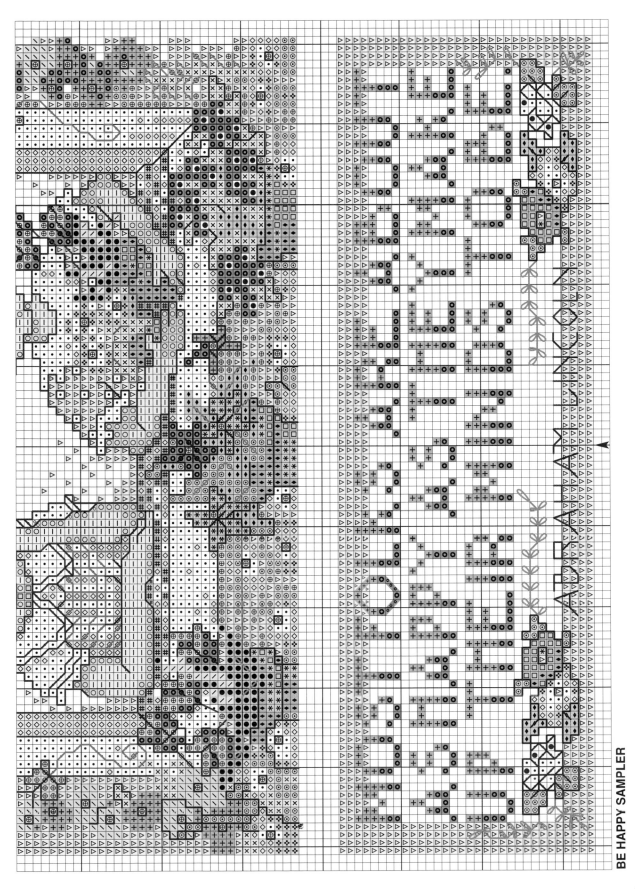

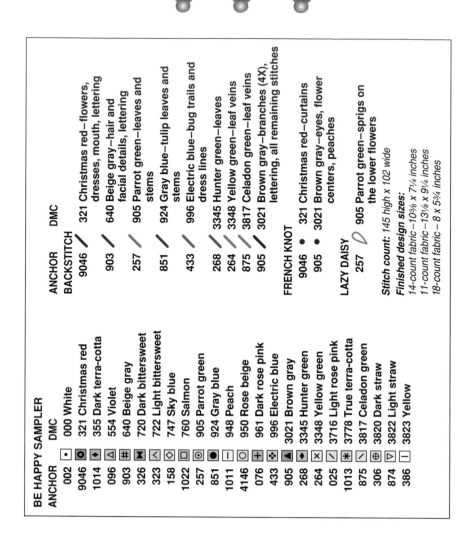

BE HAPPY SAMPLER

ANCHOR	DMC	
002	000	White
9046	321	Christmas red
1014	355	Dark terra-cotta
096	554	Violet
903	640	Beige gray
326	720	Dark bittersweet
323	722	Light bittersweet
158	747	Sky blue
1022	760	Salmon
257	905	Parrot green
851	924	Gray blue
1011	948	Peach
4146	950	Rose beige
076	961	Dark rose pink
433	996	Electric blue
905	3021	Brown gray
268	3345	Hunter green
264	3348	Yellow green
025	3716	Light rose pink
1013	3778	True terra-cotta
875	3817	Celadon green
306	3820	Dark straw
874	3822	Light straw
386	3823	Yellow

ANCHOR	DMC	
BACKSTITCH		
9046	321	Christmas red–flowers, dresses, mouth, lettering
903	640	Beige gray–hair and facial details, lettering
257	905	Parrot green–leaves and stems
851	924	Gray blue–tulip leaves and stems
433	996	Electric blue–bug trails and dress lines
268	3345	Hunter green–leaves
264	3348	Yellow green–leaf veins
875	3817	Celadon green–leaf veins
905	3021	Brown gray–branches (4X), lettering, all remaining stitches
FRENCH KNOT		
9046	321	Christmas red–curtains
905	3021	Brown gray–eyes, flower centers, peaches
LAZY DAISY		
257	905	Parrot green–sprigs on the lower flowers

Stitch count: 145 high x 102 wide
Finished design sizes:
14-count fabric–10⅜ x 7¼ inches
11-count fabric–13⅛ x 9¼ inches
18-count fabric–8 x 5¾ inches

BE HAPPY SAMPLER

Stitch this inspiration and frame it for a place where you need a reminder (shown on page 39). Finished design is 10⅜×7¼ inches.

MATERIALS
FABRIC
16×13-inch piece of 28-count pale yellow Annabelle fabric
THREADS
Cotton embroidery floss in colors listed in the key above
Two additional skeins of DMC 3822 and white
One additional skein of DMC 747, 3021, and 3823

SUPPLIES
Needle; embroidery hoop
Frame and mat of choice

INSTRUCTIONS
Tape or zigzag edges of fabric to prevent fraying. Find the center of the chart and the center of the linen. Begin stitching there.

Work cross-stitches using three plies of floss over two threads of the Annabelle fabric. Use two plies of embroidery floss to work the backstitches, lazy daisy stitches, and French knots.

Press finished stitchery on the wrong side with a warm iron.

Frame and mat as desired.

HOLLYHOCK PICTURE MAT

Butterflies and honeybees visit the flowers that frame a favorite photo (shown on page 38). Finished mat is 6¼×8½ inches.

MATERIALS
FABRIC
12×14-inch piece of 25-count light tan Dublin cloth
THREADS
Cotton embroidery floss in colors listed in the key on page 45

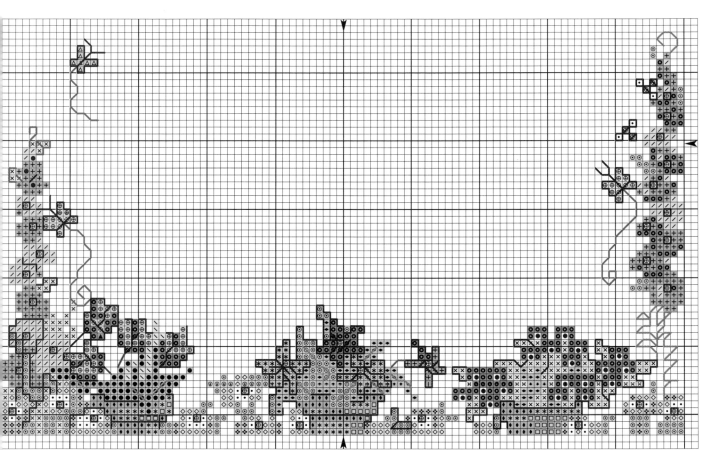

HOLLYHOCK PICTURE MAT

SUPPLIES

Needle
Embroidery hoop
Tracing paper
6¼×8½-inch piece of mat board
10×14-inch piece of fusible fleece
½ yard of ⅛-inch-wide gold braid
Crafts glue

INSTRUCTIONS

Tape or zigzag the edges of the fabric to prevent fraying. Find the center of the bottom edge of the chart and the center of the 14-inch side of the Dublin cloth. Begin stitching at this center point, 3½ inches above the edge of the Dublin cloth.

Work cross-stitches using three plies of floss over two threads of the Dublin cloth. Use two plies of

HOLLYHOCK PICTURE MAT

ANCHOR		DMC	
002	⊡	000	White
9046	◉	321	Christmas red
1014	◆	355	Dark terra-cotta
096	△	554	Violet
158	◇	747	Sky blue
1022	▢	760	Salmon
257	◉	905	Parrot green
851	●	924	Gray blue
076	✚	961	Dark rose pink
433	✤	996	Electric blue
905	▲	3021	Brown gray
268	◆	3345	Hunter green
264	✕	3348	Yellow green
025	⟋	3716	Light rose pink
1013	✳	3778	True terra-cotta
875	◟	3817	Celadon green
306	⊕	3820	Dark straw

BACKSTITCH

9046	⟋	321	Christmas red–flowers

ANCHOR		DMC	
BACKSTITCH			
257	⟋	905	Parrot green–leaves and stems
851	⟋	924	Gray blue–tulip stems
433	⟋	996	Electric blue–bug trails
268	⟋	3345	Hunter green–leaves
264	⟋	3348	Yellow green–leaf veins
875	⟋	3817	Celadon green–leaf veins
905	⟋	3021	Brown gray–all remaining stitches
FRENCH KNOT			
905	●	3021	Brown gray–flower centers

Stitch count: 59 high x 100 wide
Finished design sizes:
14-count fabric – 4¼ x 7⅛ inches
11-count fabric – 5⅜ x 9⅛ inches
18-count fabric – 3¼ x 5½ inches

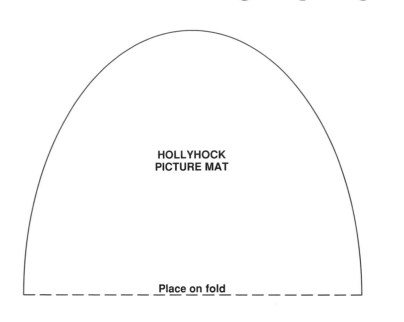

HOLLYHOCK
PICTURE MAT

Place on fold

floss to work the backstitches and French knots.

Trace the oval pattern provided above. Cut out oval pattern and center on mat board, 1½ inches from each side, 2 inches above bottom, and ¾ inch below top. Cut oval out of mat board.

Trim the Dublin cloth to 7¼×9½ inches, trimming 1 inch from the edge of stitching on sides and bottom.

Center a 6¼×8½-inch piece of fusible fleece on the back of the stitchery and fuse in place. Glue a second 6¼×8½-inch piece of fleece to the mat board. Cut oval opening in fleece.

Pull ½ inch of Dublin cloth to back of mat board on all four sides and glue in place. Fold and miter corners to make them smooth.

Trim Dublin cloth, from the back, for oval opening, leaving ½-inch allowance. Clip notches in Dublin cloth at ¼-inch intervals around the oval. Glue clipped fabric allowance to back of mat board.

Glue the gold braid around the oval shape.

ORANGE GROVE MIRROR

Check your smile with this dainty hand mirror embellished with the sweetness of tree-ripened fruit (shown on page 38). Finished mirror insert is 3½ inches in diameter.

MATERIALS
FABRIC
9×9-inch piece of 25-count white Dublin cloth
THREADS
Cotton embroidery floss in colors listed in the key on page 47
SUPPLIES
Needle; embroidery hoop
Hand mirror with 3½-inch-diameter insert opening
8×4-inch piece of fusible fleece
½ yard of ⅛-inch-diameter white cord
Crafts glue

INSTRUCTIONS
Tape or zigzag edges of fabric to prevent fraying. Find the center of the chart and the center of fabric. Begin stitching there.

Work cross-stitches using three plies of floss over two threads of the Dublin cloth. Use two plies of floss to work the backstitches and French knots.

Cut two circles of fusible fleece, using the insert pattern supplied with the mirror.

Fuse fleece to wrong side of stitchery with design centered. Lightly glue the other fleece circle to the cardboard insert supplied with the mirror.

Trim cross-stitched fabric around circle, leaving a ½-inch allowance. Clip notches in allowance at ½-inch intervals. Place stitched fabric on top of cardboard insert, with the two layers of fleece together. Glue clipped Dublin cloth edges to back of cardboard. Insert in mirror.

Place cording around edge of insert, butting ends together. Secure with a small amount of glue.

PRIMROSE TABLE MAT

For a well-dressed, inviting summer table, center a pot of flowers on this mat (shown on page 40). Finished mat is a 15½-inch square.

MATERIALS
FABRICS
16×16-inch piece of 25-count dirty linen Dublin cloth
½ yard of pink cotton fabric
THREADS
Cotton embroidery floss in colors listed in the key on page 47
SUPPLIES
Needle
Embroidery hoop
1¾ yards of ¼-inch-wide decorative trim

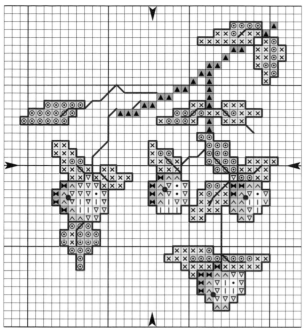

ORANGE GROVE MIRROR

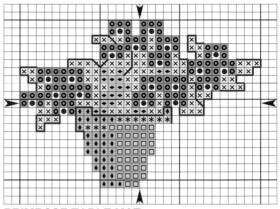

PRIMROSE TABLE MAT

ORANGE GROVE MIRROR

ANCHOR		DMC	
002	·	000	White
326	⋈	720	Dark bittersweet
323	△	722	Light bittersweet
257	⊙	905	Parrot green
905	▲	3021	Brown gray
264	✕	3348	Yellow green
874	▽	3822	Straw
386	▯	3823	Yellow

BACKSTITCH

905	/	3021	Brown gray– all stitches

FRENCH KNOT

905	●	3021	Brown gray– oranges

Stitch count: 36 high x 33 wide
Finished design sizes:
25-count fabric – 2⅞ x 2⅝ inches
22-count fabric – 3¼ x 3 inches
36-count fabric – 2 x 1⅞ inches

INSTRUCTIONS

Tape or zigzag edges of fabric to prevent fraying. Find the center of one side of the fabric and mark with a basting thread. One flowerpot will be stitched on each side of this point, leaving two stitches between the motifs. Measure 3 inches from edge of fabric and mark with a basting thread. The bottom of the flowerpots will be stitched on this line. Match these two identified lines to the bottom and one side of the flowerpot motif on the chart to position cross-stitching. Repeat for the other three sides of fabric.

Work cross-stitches using three plies of floss over two threads of the fabric. Use two plies of floss to work the backstitches and the French knots.

Press finished stitchery on the wrong side with a warm iron.

Trim fabric to a 12-inch square, trimming 1 inch below bottom of flowerpots.

Cut four 3×16½-inch strips of pink fabric. Cut one 16½-inch square of pink fabric.

Stitch pink border strips to Dublin cloth, using ½-inch seams and mitering corners. Stitch decorative trim to outer edges of all four sides, leaving a ½-inch allowance.

Place pink backing on top of front with right sides together. Stitch on top of stitching line for

PRIMROSE TABLE MAT

ANCHOR		DMC	
002	·	000	White
9046	⊙	321	Christmas red
1014	◆	355	Dark terra-cotta
1022	▢	760	Salmon
268	◖	3345	Hunter green
264	✕	3348	Yellow green
1013	✳	3778	True terra-cotta

BACKSTITCH

905	/	3021	Brown gray– all stitches

FRENCH KNOT

905	●	3021	Brown gray–flower centers

Stitch count: 21 high x 30 wide
Finished design sizes:
25-count fabric – 1⅝ x 2⅜ inches
22-count fabric – 1⅞ x 2¾ inches
36-count fabric – 1⅛ x 1⅝ inches

decorative trim, leaving an opening for turning.

Clip corners and turn right side out. Whipstitch the opening closed.

TOPSY-TURVY DOLL—BRUNETTE GIRL

TOPSY-TURVY DOLL—BLOND GIRL

TOPSY-TURVY DOLL— BRUNETTE GIRL

ANCHOR		DMC	
002	•	000	White
9046	◉	321	Christmas red
1014	◆	355	Dark terra-cotta
903	⊞	640	Beige gray
158	◇	747	Sky blue
1022	☐	760	Salmon
851	●	924	Gray blue
1011	–	948	Peach
4146	○	950	Rose beige
433	✪	996	Electric blue
905	▲	3021	Brown gray
268	◖	3345	Hunter green
264	✕	3348	Yellow green
1013	✻	3778	True terra-cotta
875	◣	3817	Celadon green
306	⊕	3820	Dark straw
874	▽	3822	Light straw

BACKSTITCH

9046	╱	321	Christmas red–dress
903	╱	640	Beige gray–hair and facial details
851	╱	924	Gray blue–tulip leaves and stems
905	╱	3021	Brown gray–all remaining stitches

FRENCH KNOT

905	•	3021	Brown gray–eyes

Stitch count: 38 high x 35 wide
Finished design sizes:
25-count fabric – 3⅛ x 2⅞ inches
22-count fabric – 3⅜ x 3⅛ inches
36-count fabric – 2⅛ x 1⅞ inches

TOPSY-TURVY DOLL— BLOND GIRL

ANCHOR		DMC	
002	•	000	White
9046	◉	321	Christmas red
158	◇	747	Sky blue
1022	☐	760	Salmon
1011	–	948	Peach
4146	○	950	Rose beige
076	✛	961	Dark rose pink
874	▽	3822	Light straw
386	☐	3823	Yellow

BACKSTITCH

9046	╱	321	Christmas red–dress and mouth
903	╱	640	Beige gray–eyebrows
433	╱	996	Electric blue–dress lines
905	╱	3021	Brown gray–all remaining stitches

FRENCH KNOT

905	•	3021	Brown gray–eyes

Stitch count: 37 high x 30 wide
Finished design sizes:
14-count fabric –2⅝ x 2⅛ inches
11-count fabric –3⅜ x 2¾ inches
18-count fabric –2⅛ x 1⅝ inches

TOPSY-TURVY DOLL

Help a little girl find a smile with this little doll (shown on page 41).
Finished doll is 7½ inches tall.

MATERIALS
FABRICS
12×12-inch piece of 25-count cream Lugana cloth
5×23-inch piece of yellow fabric
5×23-inch piece of blue fabric
THREADS
Cotton embroidery floss in colors listed in the keys at left
SUPPLIES
Needle; embroidery hoop
One ¼-inch-diameter button
Polyester fiberfill
⅔ yard of ¼-inch-wide decorative trim for bottom edge
⅔ yard of ¼-inch-wide trim for skirt border
1½ yards baby rickrack
1 yard of ⅛-inch-wide satin ribbon

INSTRUCTIONS

Cut Lugana cloth in half for two 12×6-inch pieces.

Tape or zigzag edges of one piece of the Lugana cloth to prevent fraying. Mark the center of one piece of the Lugana cloth (3 inches from each side) with a basting thread. Find the center of the chart for one girl. Begin stitching the first girl so the top of the head will be 2 inches below top edge of Lugana cloth.

Work cross-stitches using three plies of floss over two threads of the Lugana cloth. Use two plies of floss to work the backstitches and French knots.

Turn stitching upside down. Begin stitching the second girl centered on basting line, leaving a 1-inch unstitched space between the two charted designs.

Stitch a small button to the neck of the dress on the blond girl. Trim Lugana cloth around stitching, leaving ¾ inch for the finishing.

Use the trimmed stitchery as a pattern to cut a backing piece from remaining Lugana cloth.

Place backing fabric on top of cross-stitched fabric with right sides together. Stitch around outer edge, using ½-inch seam, leaving an opening in one side for turning and stuffing. Clip seams at curves.

Turn and stuff firmly with polyester fiberfill. Whipstitch the opening closed.

Stitch decorative trim ½ inch from one long edge of yellow skirt fabric. Place blue skirt fabric on top of the yellow, with right sides together. Sew the two pieces together along stitching line where trim was attached.

Press skirt open and stitch trimmings 1¼ inches from seam, using baby rickrack on one side and ¼-inch-wide trim on the other. Stitch ends together with a ½-inch seam, forming a circle.

Turn under raw edges of the top (yellow fabric) and the bottom (blue fabric) and gather them separately to fit the center of the doll. Whipstitch each gathered skirt below the cross-stitching.

Tie baby rickrack around waist of one side and make a bow. Tie the satin ribbon around other side and make a bow. Tie a small satin bow and tack it in the hair of the brunette girl.

Breit Ideas

Happy are the hands that find more stitching projects from this cheerful design.

❦ Flowerpots from the Primrose Table Mat chart add summer spirit to pockets and lapels of casual cotton clothing. Use waste canvas or a cross-stitch band to embellish wearables. Add shine by using beads in place of the French knots.

❦ Sunglasses will never get lost when you stitch your own case with hollyhocks. Use the right side of the Hollyhock Picture Mat to create a slipcover so your shades will have it made.

❦ Stitch the sampler for your sister using this Be Happy pattern. Substitute your names in the space devoted to the quotation, or personalize it further with a family saying.

❦ Kitchen-fresh stitchery features orange tree boughs loaded with fruit. Use the Orange Grove Mirror chart to cross-stitch on a prefinished hot pad or an apron. Stitch over one thread of 18-count fabric for coasters.

❦ Patchwork created with 4-inch blocks of red-checked fabric and flowerpots stitched on Aida cloth can be used for a country-style pillow top.

❦ Stitch the flowerpots on 6-count fabric for a cheery window treatment. Use good-sized bright-colored beads in place of the French knots.

COMFORT
ONE ANOTHER

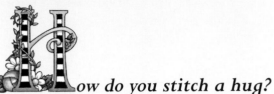

ow do you stitch a hug? It's charted for you in this chapter, along with sunshine, flowers, honeybees, bunnies, and other symbols of comfort. You'll find peace when you stitch this sunshine-washed design.

LOVE COMFORTETH
LIKE SUNSHINE
AFTER RAIN. WILLIAM SHAKESPEARE

*ike sunshine, this Mary
Engelbreit design, opposite, makes you feel better. Busy and alive with
buzzing bees, a scampering squirrel, a swimming swan, a hopping bunny, and
blooming flowers, the warm scene prompts a feeling of serenity.*

*Stitched with an elegant swan, embellished with lace, and tied with ribbon,
this covered hanger, above, has all the elements of luxury.*

*his pincushion, above, makes a
lovely reminder of the universal, timeless message that "Love comforteth."*

*Border your bed linens, opposite, top left, with delicate blooms for sweet
dreams. The cross-stitch band provides endless decorating opportunities.
A few beads add a dewdrop gleam to an old-fashioned flowered
bookmark, opposite. Elegant and easy to make, it is stitched on paper,
backed with suede, and embellished with a silky tassel.*

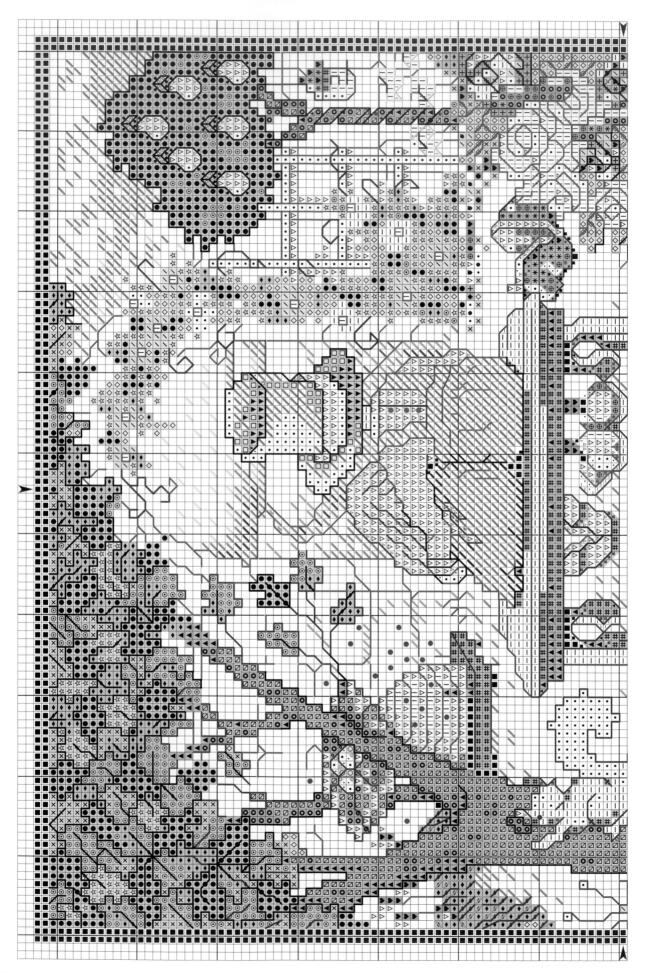

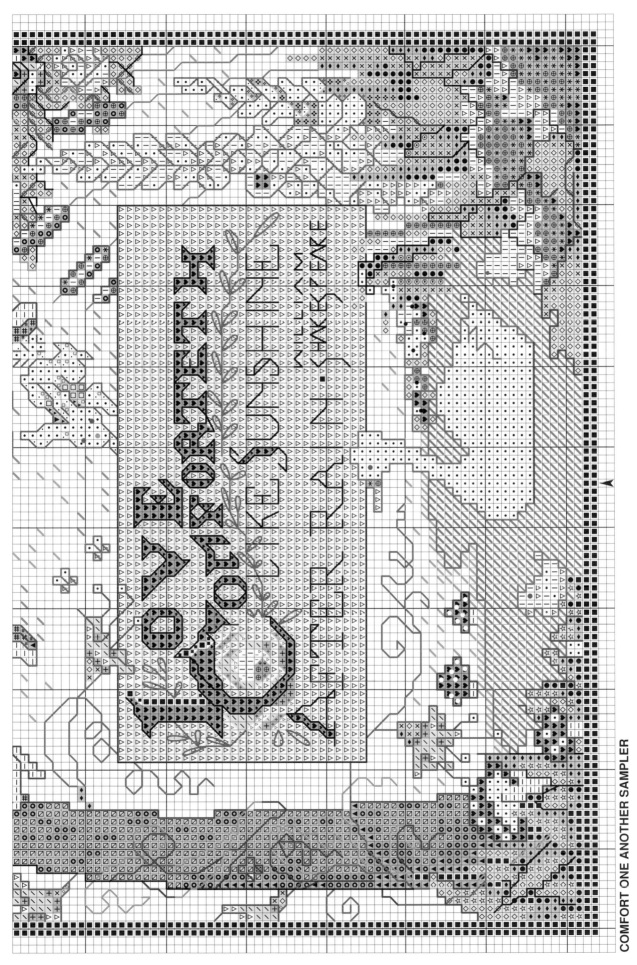

COMFORT ONE ANOTHER SAMPLER

ANCHOR	DMC		
387		Ecru	
002	000	White	
403	310	Black	
013	349	Dark coral	
011	350	Medium coral	
288	445	Lemon	
683	500	Blue green	
273	645	Dark beaver gray	
900	648	Light beaver gray	
226	702	Christmas green	
295	726	Light topaz	
280	733	Olive	
314	741	Tangerine	
309	781	Dark topaz	
168	807	Peacock blue	
161	826	Bright blue	
360	839	Dark beige brown	
379	840	Medium beige brown	
258	904	Deep parrot green	
256	906	Medium parrot green	
255	907	Light parrot green	
340	920	Copper	
076	961	Dark rose pink	
025	3716	Light rose pink	

HALF CROSS-STITCH
(stitch in direction of symbol)

ANCHOR	DMC	
002	000	White
011	350	Medium coral
288	445	Lemon
295	726	Light topaz
280	733	Olive
168	807	Peacock blue
256	906	Medium parrot green
255	907	Light parrot green
076	961	Dark rose pink
328	3341	Melon
025	3716	Light rose pink

BACKSTITCH

ANCHOR	DMC	
002	000	White—girl's dress, girl's hair
013	349	Dark coral—boy's hat, boy's shirt, girl's shoes, flowers, bird feeder
011	350	Medium coral—motto border
683	500	Blue green—tree leaves, grass, vines on trellis, bottom of swan
273	645	Dark beaver gray—dress outline, boy's pants, trellis, rabbit, blue foxglove flowers, horizon
226	702	Christmas green—rose leaves
295	726	Light topaz—flowers
280	733	Olive—motto panel
314	741	Tangerine—duck bill, cottontail stems, flowers
309	781	Dark topaz—beehive, trellis, stone wall, road, girl's hair, boy's shirt, boy's shoes, flowers, swan, ducks
168	807	Peacock blue—boy's pants
360	839	Dark beige brown—tree, tree leaves, nest, beehive base, squirrel, bench, girl's shoes, girl's hair, boy's shoes, bird feeder, cottontails, mushrooms, grass
379	840	Medium beige brown—bench
258	904	Deep parrot green—flower stems, flower vines, grass
256	906	Medium parrot green—flower vines, rose leaves
256	907	Light parrot green—grass, vines
340	920	Copper—trumpet flowers
403	310	Black—lettering (2X); all remaining stitches

LAZY DAISY

ANCHOR	DMC	
280	733	Olive—motto panel

FRENCH KNOT

ANCHOR	DMC	
002	000	White—mushrooms
403	310	Black—flower centers, ladybug
273	645	Dark beaver gray—rabbit, duck, swan eyes
360	839	Dark beige brown—squirrel's eye
379	840	Medium beige brown—bees
025	3716	Light rose pink—rabbit's nose

Stitch count: 147 high x 113 wide

Finished design sizes:
11-count fabric – 10½ x 8⅛ inches
11-count fabric – 13⅜ x 10¼ inches
18-count fabric – 8⅛ x 6¼ inches

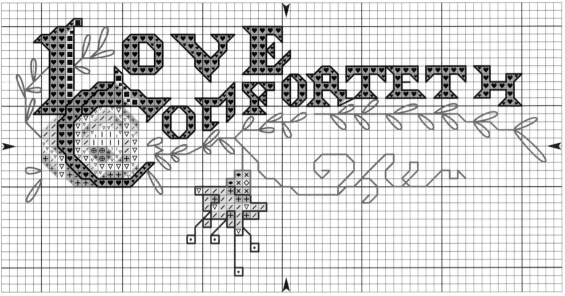

PINCUSHION

COMFORT ONE ANOTHER SAMPLER

Enjoy the peacefulness of this sunshine-filled scene (shown on page 52).
Finished design is 11×8½ inches.

MATERIALS
FABRIC
18×15-inch piece of 14-count baby yellow Aida cloth
THREADS
Cotton embroidery floss in colors listed in the key on page 58
Two additional skeins of DMC 726
One additional skein of DMC 310 and 781
SUPPLIES
Needle; embroidery hoop
Frame and mat of choice

INSTRUCTIONS
Tape or zigzag edges of fabric to prevent fraying. Find the center of the chart and the center of the fabric. Begin stitching there.

Work the cross-stitches and half cross-stitches using three plies of embroidery floss. Use two plies of embroidery floss to work the backstitches, French knots, and lazy daisy stitches.

Press finished stitchery on the wrong side with a warm iron.

Frame and mat as desired.

PINCUSHION

Although it is useful, this lovely reminder deserves to be on display (shown on page 54).
Finished pincushion is a 2¾×4½-inch oval.

MATERIALS
FABRIC
7×9-inch piece of 36-count cream Edinborough linen
THREADS
Cotton embroidery floss in colors listed in the key at right
SUPPLIES
Needle
Embroidery hoop
2¾×4½-inch oval Shaker pincushion
⅓ yard of ½-inch-wide lace
Tacky glue

PINCUSHION		
ANCHOR		**DMC**
002	·	000 White
403	■	310 Black
013	♥	349 Dark coral
288	Ι	445 Lemon
295	▽	726 Light topaz
314	⊕	741 Tangerine
258	◆	904 Deep parrot green
256	✕	906 Medium parrot green
255	◇	907 Light parrot green
076	+	961 Dark rose pink
025	∕	3716 Light rose pink
BACKSTITCH		
013	╱	349 Coral—trumpet flower
280	╱	733 Olive—vine
258	╱	904 Deep parrot green—flower stem, flower vine
403	╱	310 Black—all remaining stitches
LAZY DAISY		
280	⟋	733 Olive—leaves

Stitch count: 32 high x 66 wide
Finished design sizes:
36-count fabric – 1¾ x 3¾ inches
22-count fabric – 2⅞ x 6 inches
28-count fabric – 2¼ x 4¾ inches

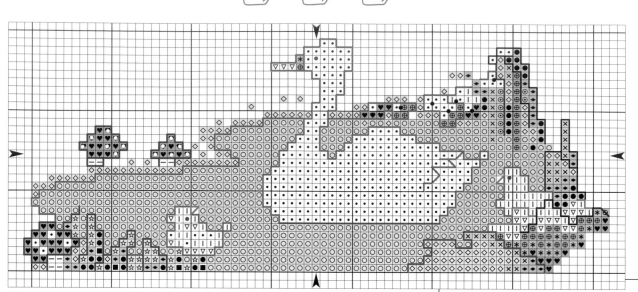

SWAN CLOTHES HANGER

INSTRUCTIONS

Tape or zigzag edges of linen to prevent fraying. Find center of the chart and center of the linen. Begin stitching there.

Work cross-stitches using two plies of floss over two threads of the linen. Use two plies to work the backstitches and lazy daisy stitches.

Press stitchery on the wrong side with a warm iron.

Trim the linen, using the pattern supplied with pincushion. Follow manufacturer's directions to cover the top of the pincushion.

Add lace trim around edge using a small amount of glue, or tack in place with needle and thread.

SWAN CLOTHES HANGER

Any item will be special hanging on this covered clothes hanger (shown on page 53).
Finished hanger is 8×14 inches.

MATERIALS

FABRICS
10×18-inch piece of 18-count carnation pink damask Aida cloth
8×16-inch piece of fabric of choice for backing
8×16-inch piece of fleece

THREADS
Cotton embroidery floss in colors listed in the key at right

SUPPLIES
Needle; embroidery hoop
Child's plastic coat hanger
¾ yard of ¼-inch-wide lace edging
1 yard gathered 1¾-inch-wide lace edging
2 yards of ¼-inch-wide picot-edged satin ribbon

SWAN CLOTHES HANGER

ANCHOR		DMC
387	−	Ecru
002	•	000 White
403	■	310 Black
013	♥	349 Dark coral
011	✳	350 Medium coral
288	❙	445 Lemon
683	●	500 Blue green
226	◉	702 Christmas green
295	▽	726 Light topaz
280	☆	733 Olive
314	⊕	741 Tangerine
168	◯	807 Peacock blue
258	◆	904 Deep parrot green
256	✕	906 Medium parrot green
255	◇	907 Light parrot green

BACKSTITCH

013	╱	349 Dark coral−flowers
683	╱	500 Blue green−grass
314	╱	741 Tangerine−duck bill, flowers
309	╱	781 Dark topaz−ducks
360	╱	839 Dark beige brown− mushrooms, grass
258	╱	904 Deep parrot green−lake
403	╱	310 Black−all remaining stitches

FRENCH KNOT

002	○	000 White−mushrooms
403	●	310 Black−flower centers
273	●	645 Dark beaver gray− swan's eye, ducks' eyes

Stitch count: 29 high x 73 wide
Finished design sizes:
18-count fabric − 1⅝ x 4⅛ inches
14-count fabric − 2⅛ x 5¼ inches
11-count fabric − 2⅝ x 6⅝ inches

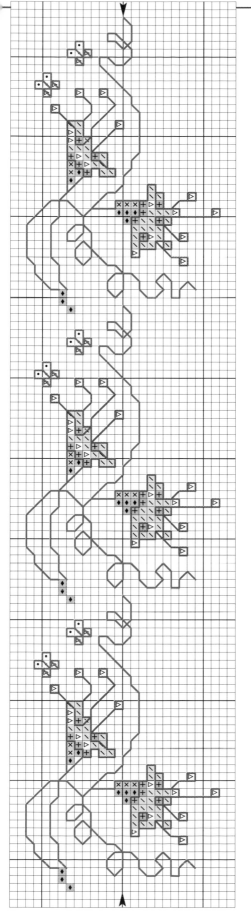

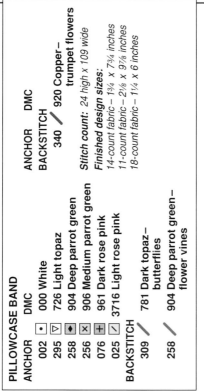

PILLOWCASE BAND		
ANCHOR	**DMC**	
002	•	000 White
295	▷	726 Light topaz
258	◆	904 Deep parrot green
256	☒	906 Medium parrot green
076	✚	961 Dark rose pink
025	◣	3716 Light rose pink
BACKSTITCH		
309	╱	781 Dark topaz – butterflies
258	╱	904 Deep parrot green – flower vines

ANCHOR	DMC	
BACKSTITCH		
340	╱	920 Copper – trumpet flowers

Stitch count: 24 high x 109 wide
Finished design sizes:
14-count fabric – 1¾ x 7¾ inches
11-count fabric – 2⅛ x 9⅞ inches
18-count fabric – 1¼ x 6 inches

INSTRUCTIONS

Tape or zigzag edges of Aida cloth to prevent fraying. Find the center of the chart and the center of the fabric. Begin stitching there.

Work cross-stitches using two plies of floss over two squares of Aida cloth. Use two plies to work the backstitches and French knots.

Make a paper pattern by drawing around hanger edge. Add 2 inches below the hanger. Add ½-inch seam allowance on all sides.

Use paper pattern to cut one piece of backing fabric and one piece of fleece. Center paper pattern over cross-stitching and cut out front of hanger cover.

Place fleece on wrong side of cross-stitched front of hanger cover. Baste fleece to Aida cloth around outside edge.

Stitch ¼-inch-wide lace edging to top and sides of the hanger front.

Stitch ¼-inch-wide lace edging to top of neck of fabric for backing. Stitch back to front with right sides together, leaving neck at top and bottom edges open.

Turn up a narrow hem along lower edge of hanger cover and stitch, adding the 1¾-inch gathered lace edging.

Wrap hanger top with ribbon, gluing it in place to cover hanger. Tie ribbon in a large bow at neck of hanger. Slip cover over hanger.

PILLOWCASE BAND

Fanciful flowers add finery to bed linens. Ours grace a pillowcase band (shown on page 55). Finished band is 2½×40 inches.

MATERIALS

FABRICS
1¼ yards of 2½-inch-wide 14-count yellow-edged cross-stitch band
Pillowcase of choice or 1 yard of fabric to make a pillowcase

THREADS
Cotton embroidery floss in colors listed in the key above left

SUPPLIES
Needle
2½ yards of ¾-inch-wide lace edging
Matching sewing thread

INSTRUCTIONS

Find the center of the chart and the center of the cross-stitch band. Begin stitching there.

Work cross-stitches using three plies of floss. Use two plies to work the backstitches.

Repeat stitching chart to make the band fit the pillowcase.

Trim the cross-stitch band 1 inch longer than circumference of the pillowcase. With the right sides together, stitch a ½-inch seam to join the band into a circle.

Stitch lace edging and cross-stitch band along the open edge of the pillowcase.

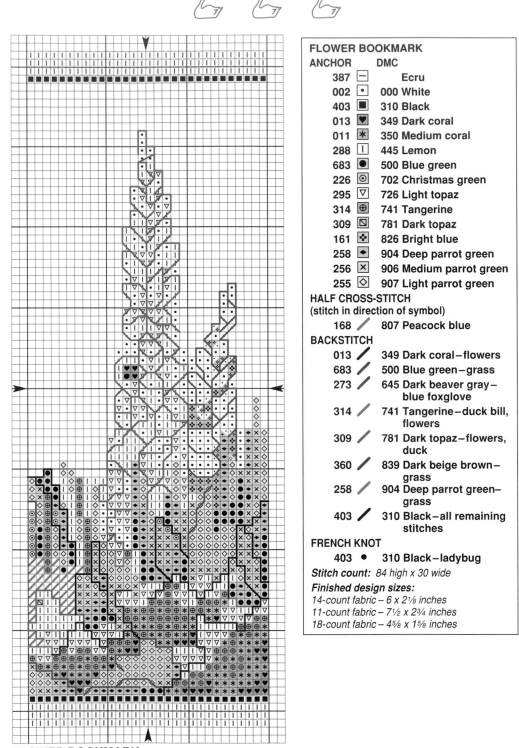

FLOWER BOOKMARK

ANCHOR		DMC	
387	⊟		Ecru
002	⊡	000	White
403	■	310	Black
013	♥	349	Dark coral
011	✳	350	Medium coral
288	⌶	445	Lemon
683	●	500	Blue green
226	⊙	702	Christmas green
295	▽	726	Light topaz
314	⊕	741	Tangerine
309	◨	781	Dark topaz
161	✤	826	Bright blue
258	◆	904	Deep parrot green
256	✕	906	Medium parrot green
255	◇	907	Light parrot green

HALF CROSS-STITCH
(stitch in direction of symbol)

168	╱	807	Peacock blue

BACKSTITCH

013	╱	349	Dark coral—flowers
683	╱	500	Blue green—grass
273	╱	645	Dark beaver gray—blue foxglove
314	╱	741	Tangerine—duck bill, flowers
309	╱	781	Dark topaz—flowers, duck
360	╱	839	Dark beige brown—grass
258	╱	904	Deep parrot green—grass
403	╱	310	Black—all remaining stitches

FRENCH KNOT

403	●	310	Black—ladybug

Stitch count: 84 high x 30 wide

Finished design sizes:
14-count fabric – 6 x 2⅛ inches
11-count fabric – 7½ x 2¾ inches
18-count fabric – 4⅝ x 1⅝ inches

FLOWER BOOKMARK

FLOWER BOOKMARK

A peaceful, old-fashioned garden is brought to mind by this bookmark (shown on page 55). Finished size is 7×2⅜ inches, not including tassel.

MATERIALS
FABRIC
8×3-inch piece of 14-count cream perforated paper
THREADS
Cotton embroidery floss in colors listed in the key on page 62
SUPPLIES
Needle
25 pearl and 21 yellow seed beads
8×3-inch piece of felted imitation suede fabric
Pinking scissors; tacky crafts glue
3-inch tassel of choice

INSTRUCTIONS
Find center of chart and of perforated paper. Begin stitching there.

Work cross-stitches using three plies of floss over one square of the perforated paper. Use two plies of floss to work the half cross-stitches, backstitches, and French knots, and to attach the beads. Attach pearl beads randomly to tall yellow flowers. Attach yellow beads randomly to short yellow flowers.

Trim perforated paper 1 inch above top of stitching and 1 row beyond other stitched edges. Trim the top to a point.

Cut a 7¼×2⅜-inch piece of the suede fabric with pinking scissors. Trim corners away at top.

Center cross-stitched perforated paper on suede fabric. Use a small amount of crafts glue under the stitched areas to glue in place.

Tack loop on tassel to the top of the bookmark, sewing through suede fabric and perforated paper.

Breit Ideas
Comforting, peaceful, and pleasant pictures overflow from this Mary Engelbreit design.

🦢 A wedding day remembrance could be stitched from this "Love Comforteth" design. Replace the entire quote with the names of the bride and groom and the wedding date, or leave the words and add the personalization.

🦢 Stitch a hug by isolating the boy and girl on the bench. Use the sweet stitchery to celebrate the relationship of a brother and sister or a loving couple on anything from a pillow to a greeting card.

🦢 The graceful swan is a serene bathroom motif. Stitch it on a towel with an Aida cloth insert, make it into a sachet, or use it for a box lid or hand mirror.

🦢 Move beyond borders by stitching the perimeter of this design. Begin at the lower right corner of the design with the flower garden, move across the bottom with the swan, climb the big tree, and come down the right side with the pear tree and flowers. This unique outline could frame a personal message or be turned into a lovely padded mat for a photo or mirror.

🦢 Stitch love into baby gifts with the many little motifs from this design. Use prefinished bibs, towels, and other baby wear; stitch directly on thermal knits; or dress up waste canvas to add a personal touch to a gift. A bunny, squirrel, swan, or flower makes a baby undershirt special.

🦢 Delicate flowers from the pillowcase chart make lovely embellishments for home decorating and wearables. Stitch these light flower vines on a shirt pocket, a sachet, an eyeglasses case, or a curtain tieback.

HELPING HANDS

weet remembrances grow from good service and from the hands that cross-stitch. If your hands are too busy to take on a big project, you'll find this design lends itself to some quick-growing projects.

SOW GOOD SERVICES:
SWEET REMEMBRANCES
WILL GROW FROM THEM.

Mde. de Stael

SWEET
REMEMBRANCES

et into a garden party
frame of mind by dressing an ordinary straw hat,
above left, *with a band of flowers. Gingham checks
on a doily,* above, *brighten any setting.*

Mary Engelbreit's design, opposite, *answers the
question "How does your garden grow?" with
sunshine. Lazy daisy stitches on a yellow cross-
stitched border frame this garden of hearts.*

emember your guests with this
personal welcome, **above**. The cheerful linen hand towel and little scented
pillow adorn a nightstand or bed as they convey their sentimental
message. Both items make charming gifts.

Check out how well checked fabric complements the homey design and
message, **opposite**. Choose ruffles to coordinate with your decor as you perk
up a corner in your home with this gentle thought made into a soft pillow.
Memories are made of projects like these.

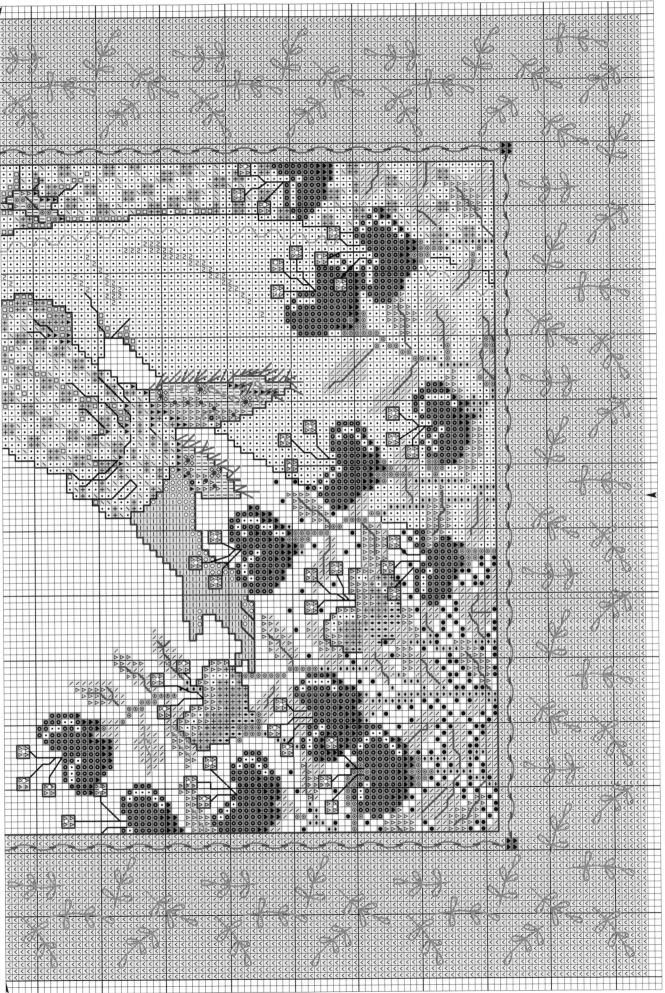

HELPING HANDS SAMPLER

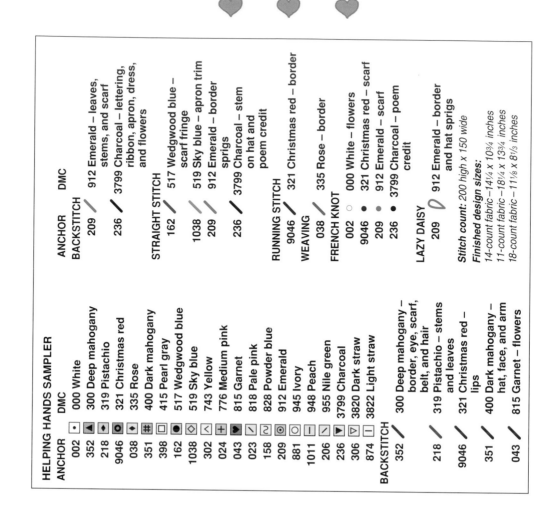

HELPING HANDS SAMPLER

ANCHOR		DMC	
002	•	000	White
352	◀	300	Deep mahogany
218	◆	319	Pistachio
9046	◉	321	Christmas red
038	◆	335	Rose
351	#	400	Dark mahogany
398	□	415	Pearl gray
162	●	517	Wedgwood blue
1038	◇	519	Sky blue
302	◁	743	Yellow
024	+	776	Medium pink
043	▶	815	Garnet
023	◣	818	Pale pink
158	◿	828	Powder blue
209	◉	912	Emerald
881	○	945	Ivory
1011	|	948	Peach
206	/	955	Nile green
236	▶	3799	Charcoal
306	▷	3820	Dark straw
874	—	3822	Light straw

BACKSTITCH

ANCHOR	DMC	
352	300	Deep mahogany – border, eye, scarf, belt, and hair
218	319	Pistachio – stems and leaves
9046	321	Christmas red – lips
351	400	Dark mahogany – hat, face, and arm
043	815	Garnet – flowers

BACKSTITCH (ANCHOR / DMC)

209	912	Emerald – leaves, stems, and scarf
236	3799	Charcoal – lettering, ribbon, apron, dress, and flowers

STRAIGHT STITCH

162	517	Wedgwood blue – scarf fringe
1038	519	Sky blue – apron trim
209	912	Emerald – border sprigs
236	3799	Charcoal – stem on hat and poem credit

RUNNING STITCH

9046	321	Christmas red – border

WEAVING

038	335	Rose – border

FRENCH KNOT

002	000	White – flowers
9046	321	Christmas red – scarf
209	912	Emerald – scarf
236	3799	Charcoal – poem credit

LAZY DAISY

209	912	Emerald – border and hat sprigs

Stitch count: 200 high x 150 wide
Finished design sizes:
14-count fabric–14¼ x 10¾ inches
11-count fabric–18¼ x 13¾ inches
18-count fabric–11⅛ x 8⅓ inches

HELPING HANDS SAMPLER

Working on this design is as close as you can get to cross-stitching sunshine (shown on page 67). Finished design is 14¼×10¾ inches.

MATERIALS
FABRIC
20×16-inch piece of 14-count light blue Aida cloth
THREADS
Cotton embroidery floss in colors listed in the key above
Eight additional skeins of DMC 743
Two additional skeins of white
One additional skein of DMC 321 and 912
SUPPLIES
Needle; embroidery hoop
Frame and mat of choice

INSTRUCTIONS
Tape or zigzag edges of fabric to prevent fraying. Find the center of the chart and the center of the fabric. Begin stitching there.

Work cross-stitches using three plies of floss. Use two plies of floss to work the backstitches, straight stitches, lazy daisy stitches, running stitches, and French knots. Use three plies to weave through running stitches.

Press the finished stitchery on the wrong side with a warm iron.
Frame and mat stitched piece as desired.

FLOWER HATBAND

A prefinished border of blooming greenery takes a hat to a garden party (shown on page 66). Finished band is 2¼×23 inches.

MATERIALS
FABRIC
1 yard (or desired length) 2¼-inch-wide 14-count yellow-edged Aida cross-stitch band

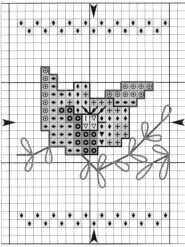

FLOWER HATBAND

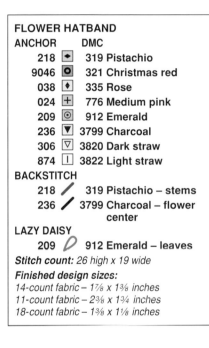

FLOWER HATBAND			
ANCHOR		DMC	
218	◆	319	Pistachio
9046	◉	321	Christmas red
038	◆	335	Rose
024	+	776	Medium pink
209	◎	912	Emerald
236	▼	3799	Charcoal
306	▽	3820	Dark straw
874	☐	3822	Light straw

BACKSTITCH

218	╱	319	Pistachio – stems
236	╱	3799	Charcoal – flower center

LAZY DAISY

209	⬭	912	Emerald – leaves

Stitch count: 26 high x 19 wide
Finished design sizes:
14-count fabric – 1⅞ x 1⅜ inches
11-count fabric – 2⅜ x 1¾ inches
18-count fabric – 1⅜ x 1⅛ inches

THREADS

Cotton embroidery floss in colors listed in the key above

SUPPLIES

Needle; embroidery hoop
White sewing thread

INSTRUCTIONS

Find the center of the chart and the center of the cross-stitch band. Begin stitching there.

Work cross-stitches using three plies of floss. Use two plies of floss to work the lazy daisy stitches and the backstitches.

Stitch checkerboard border one stitch inside woven edge of band. Repeat charted design as needed to reach desired length.

Tack hatband to hat with white sewing thread. Turn under raw edges at ends of band and whipstitch band together.

GINGHAM DOILY

Checks, fringe, and flowers combine to make a fresh table mat (shown on page 66). Finished size is 12×12 inches, including fringe.

MATERIALS

FABRIC

16×16-inch piece of 25-count white Lugana cloth

THREADS

Cotton embroidery floss in colors listed in the key on page 74

SUPPLIES

Needle
Embroidery hoop

INSTRUCTIONS

Tape or zigzag edges of fabric to prevent fraying. Mark one corner of the Lugana cloth 3¼ inches from each edge. Begin stitching the outside edge of the gingham border at that point.

Work cross-stitches using two plies of floss over two threads of the Lugana cloth. Use one ply to work the lazy daisy stitches, backstitches, and straight stitches.

Turn chart 90 degrees to repeat the pattern for each other corner.

Trim the Lugana cloth 1¼ inches outside the stitched border. Remove outer threads to make fringe.

SWEET SACHET

Remember a friend with this sweetly scented, small pillow (shown on page 68). Finished sachet is 4¾×5¾ inches.

MATERIALS

FABRIC

9×16-inch piece of 18-count white Aida cloth

THREADS

Cotton embroidery floss in colors listed in the key on page 74

SUPPLIES

Needle; embroidery hoop
¾ yard of ¼-inch-wide lace
Potpourri or other scented material

INSTRUCTIONS

Tape or zigzag edges of Aida cloth to prevent fraying. Find the center of the chart on page 75 and the center of the fabric. Begin stitching 1 inch left of the fabric center.

Work cross-stitches using two plies of floss. Use one ply of floss to work the lazy daisy stitches, French knots, backstitches, and straight stitches.

Use two plies of floss to work the running stitches over cross-stitches on the border. Use three plies of floss to weave through running stitches for border.

Center design and trim Aida cloth to a 5¼×12½-inch piece.

Stitch a ½-inch hem in both short ends of fabric. Fold the fabric with the stitching centered and right sides together (the hemmed edges will overlap). Stitch across the raw edges, making ½-inch seams through all layers, carefully following the edge of the cross-stitches. Trim seams and turn. Whipstitch lace around the edges.

Fill loosely with potpourri or other scented material.

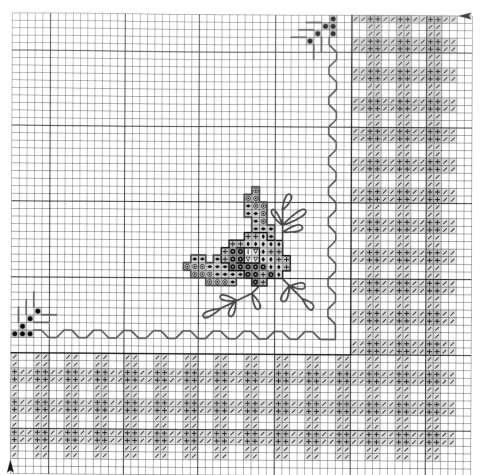

GINGHAM DOILY

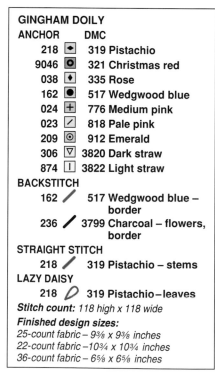

GINGHAM DOILY

ANCHOR		DMC
218	◆	319 Pistachio
9046	◎	321 Christmas red
038	◆	335 Rose
162	●	517 Wedgwood blue
024	✚	776 Medium pink
023	╱	818 Pale pink
209	◎	912 Emerald
306	▽	3820 Dark straw
874	Ⅰ	3822 Light straw

BACKSTITCH

| 162 | ╱ | 517 Wedgwood blue – border |
| 236 | ╱ | 3799 Charcoal – flowers, border |

STRAIGHT STITCH

| 218 | ╱ | 319 Pistachio – stems |

LAZY DAISY

| 218 | ⬭ | 319 Pistachio–leaves |

Stitch count: 118 high x 118 wide

Finished design sizes:
25-count fabric – 9⅜ x 9⅜ inches
22-count fabric –10¾ x 10¾ inches
36-count fabric – 6⅝ x 6⅝ inches

LINEN GUEST TOWEL

Heart flowers roll out a cheerful welcome to your home (shown on page 68).
Finished towel is 17×10 inches.

MATERIALS

FABRIC
20×14-inch piece of 28-count pastel pink linen

THREADS
Cotton embroidery floss in colors listed in the key on page 75

SUPPLIES
Needle; embroidery hoop
⅓ yard of 1-inch-wide white lace
Matching sewing thread

INSTRUCTIONS

Tape or zigzag edges of fabric to prevent fraying. Find the center of the chart and the center of a 14-inch side of the linen; measure 6 inches above the raw edge of the linen. Begin stitching there.

Work cross-stitches using two plies of floss over two threads of the linen. Use two plies to work French knots. Use one ply of floss to work the backstitches.

Repeat stitching the chart to fill the width of the towel.

Use two plies of DMC 321 to work the running stitches for the border, extending beyond the cross-stitch motifs approximately 1½ inches on each end. Using four plies of DMC 335, weave through the running stitches with an

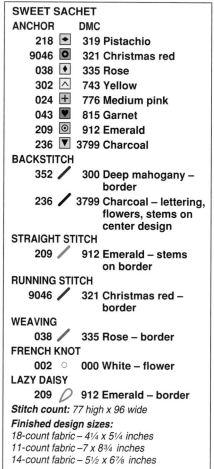

SWEET SACHET

ANCHOR		DMC
218	◖	319 Pistachio
9046	◎	321 Christmas red
038	◆	335 Rose
302	∧	743 Yellow
024	✚	776 Medium pink
043	♥	815 Garnet
209	◎	912 Emerald
236	▼	3799 Charcoal

BACKSTITCH

| 352 | ╱ | 300 Deep mahogany – border |
| 236 | ╱ | 3799 Charcoal – lettering, flowers, stems on center design |

STRAIGHT STITCH

| 209 | ╱ | 912 Emerald – stems on border |

RUNNING STITCH

| 9046 | ╱ | 321 Christmas red – border |

WEAVING

| 038 | ╱ | 335 Rose – border |

FRENCH KNOT

| 002 | ○ | 000 White – flower |

LAZY DAISY

| 209 | ⬭ | 912 Emerald – border |

Stitch count: 77 high x 96 wide

Finished design sizes:
18-count fabric – 4¼ x 5¼ inches
11-count fabric –7 x 8¾ inches
14-count fabric – 5½ x 6⅞ inches

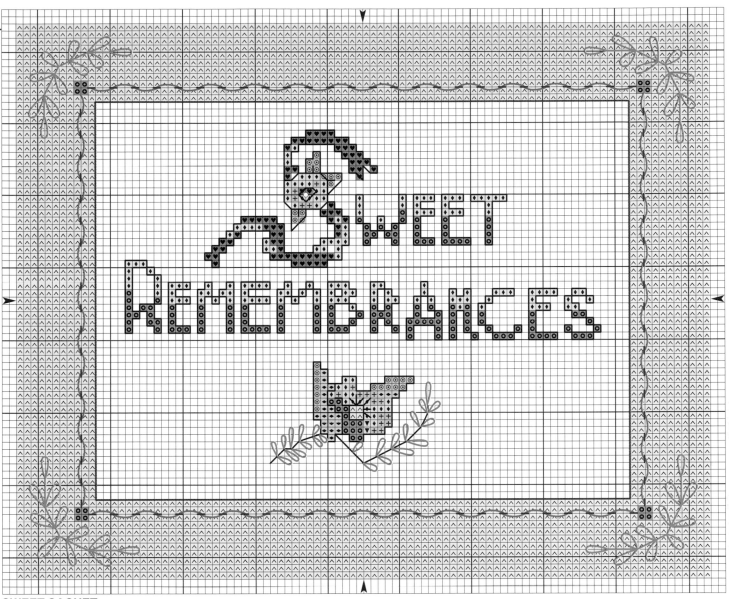

SWEET SACHET

alternating motion to create the scalloped border. Use one long piece of floss and leave the ends long and unfastened.

Trim the stitchery 4 inches below the bottom of the stitched border and 1 inch beyond stitched border on each side.

Machine-stitch a narrow hem on each side of the towel, catching the border threads into the hem. Machine-stitch a narrow hem at the unstitched end.

Turn raw edge of linen under ½ inch and whipstitch a 1¾-inch hem at the bottom. Whipstitch lace to the folded edge.

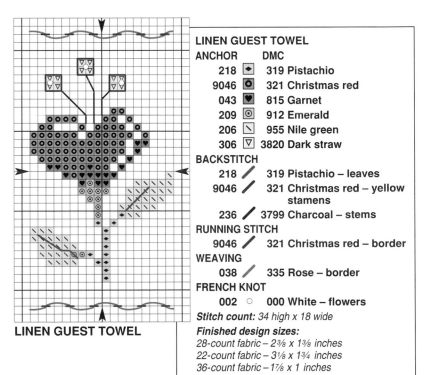

LINEN GUEST TOWEL

LINEN GUEST TOWEL

ANCHOR		DMC
218	◆	319 Pistachio
9046	◉	321 Christmas red
043	♥	815 Garnet
209	◎	912 Emerald
206	◥	955 Nile green
306	▽	3820 Dark straw

BACKSTITCH

218	╱	319 Pistachio – leaves
9046	╱	321 Christmas red – yellow stamens
236	╱	3799 Charcoal – stems

RUNNING STITCH

9046	╱	321 Christmas red – border

WEAVING

038	╱	335 Rose – border

FRENCH KNOT

002	○	000 White – flowers

Stitch count: 34 high x 18 wide

Finished design sizes:
28-count fabric – 2⅜ x 1⅜ inches
22-count fabric – 3⅛ x 1¾ inches
36-count fabric – 1⅞ x 1 inches

RUFFLED PILLOW

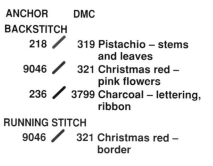

RUFFLED PILLOW

ANCHOR		DMC
002	•	000 White
218	◆	319 Pistachio
9046	◉	321 Christmas red
038	◆	335 Rose
024	+	776 Medium pink
043	♥	815 Garnet
209	◉	912 Emerald
206	◢	955 Nile green
306	▽	3820 Dark straw
874	I	3822 Light straw

ANCHOR		DMC
BACKSTITCH		
218	/	319 Pistachio – stems and leaves
9046	/	321 Christmas red – pink flowers
236	/	3799 Charcoal – lettering, ribbon
RUNNING STITCH		
9046	/	321 Christmas red – border

ANCHOR		DMC
WEAVING		
038	/	335 Rose – border
FRENCH KNOT		
002	○	000 White – flowers

Stitch count: 88 high x 86 wide
Finished design sizes:
25-count fabric – 7⅛ x 6⅞ inches
22-count fabric – 8 x 7⅞ inches
36-count fabric – 4⅞ x 4¾ inches

RUFFLED PILLOW

This gentle reminder of the value of helpfulness is highlighted with perky pink and green checked ruffles (shown on page 69). Finished pillow is 14×14 inches, including ruffles.

MATERIALS

FABRICS

14×14-inch piece of 25-count white Lugana cloth
9×9-inch piece of fleece
1 yard green checked fabric
1 yard pink checked fabric

THREADS

Cotton embroidery floss in colors listed in the key on page 76

SUPPLIES

Needle; embroidery hoop
1 yard ⅛-inch-diameter piping
8-inch square pillow form or polyester fiberfill for stuffing

INSTRUCTIONS

Tape or zigzag edges of Lugana cloth to prevent fraying. Find the center of the chart and the center of the fabric. Begin stitching there.

Work cross-stitches using two plies of floss over two threads of the Lugana cloth. Use one ply of floss to work the backstitches. Use two plies to work the French knots and the running stitches. Use three plies to weave through the running stitches to make the scalloped border.

Press finished stitchery on wrong side with a warm iron. With design centered, trim fabric to 9×9 inches.

Place the 9-inch-square piece of fleece on the back of cross-stitched piece, basting along outside edge.

Cut a 9-inch square from green checked fabric for pillow back. For green checked ruffle, cut a bias strip of fabric 7×64 inches, piecing as necessary. From pink checked fabric,

cut a 1¼×33-inch bias strip (piecing as necessary) to cover piping. Also cut a 6×64-inch bias strip (piecing as necessary) for the ruffle.

Sew short ends of piping strips together to form a continuous circle. Cut a 32-inch length of cording; center lengthwise on wrong side of pink checked piping strip with ends of cording touching. Fold fabric around cording, raw edges together. Use a zipper foot to sew through both fabric layers close to cording. Pin cording to the pillow front with raw edges even. Stitch in place.

Sew the pink checked ruffle strips together to form a circle. Fold the

strips, wrong sides together, and press fold line. Sew a gathering thread through both layers of ruffle ½ inch from raw edges. Pull threads to fit perimeter of pillow front with raw edges even; adjust gathers evenly. Sew ruffle to pillow along piping stitching line.

Repeat ruffle instructions to make the wider green checked ruffle.

Sew pillow front to back, right sides facing, keeping ruffle tucked inside. Leave an opening for turning. Clip the corners, turn right side out, and press.

Insert pillow form or stuff firmly. Slip-stitch the opening closed.

Breit Ideas

Great projects just grow from this Mary Engelbreit design.

♥ Once you've tried this easy laced border, you'll be tempted to use it again and again. Hem gingham fabric squares for napkins and add this quick-to-stitch border (using the checks as the guide for your running stitches). Have fun with mix-and-match colors to create a great summer table setting.

♥ Heart flowers can bloom on a valentine card or a ring bearer's pillow.

♥ A soft wall hanging easily could replace a mat and frame for your stitched design. Omit the yellow cross-stitches and lazy daisy stitches and border your piece with gingham sashing strips. Add batting and backing, and quilt in the ditch around your border pieces. Bind as you would a quilt. Add ribbon loops for hanging.

♥ Embellish linens for a darling doll bed or cradle with pieces and parts of the charts in this chapter. Use the gingham checked cross-stitch border (from the fringed doily) to border doll blankets. Or, stitch a border of solid cross-stitches and add lazy daisy stitches atop (as in the border of the main piece).

BROTHERLY LOVE

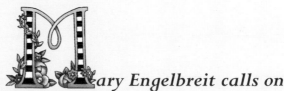

ary Engelbreit calls on the real and imagined adventures of her sons and their dog in this warm and fuzzy reminder of youth for the kid in all of us.

nnocence is captured in this
*Mary Engelbreit "young West" design, opposite. Preserve that mischievous
spirit and the happy days of youth with this nostalgic stitchery.*

*Rope tricks call attention to a favorite photo, but this frame, above, is no trick
at all when you use one of the kits available for making padded fabric frames.
A frame is just the beginning for this border: Substitute it for the one shown
on page 82 to make a vertical cover for an album.*

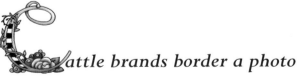

attle brands border a photo
album, *above, or scrapbook of childhood memories. Title a young dude's
ranch, name the characters, add a cross-stitched pooch, or let your creativity
shine as you put your own brand on the book.*

*Delight your favorite little buckaroo with cross-stitches on his or her duds,
opposite. You'll find many more elements in the charts that can be
used for do-it-yourself Western wear.*

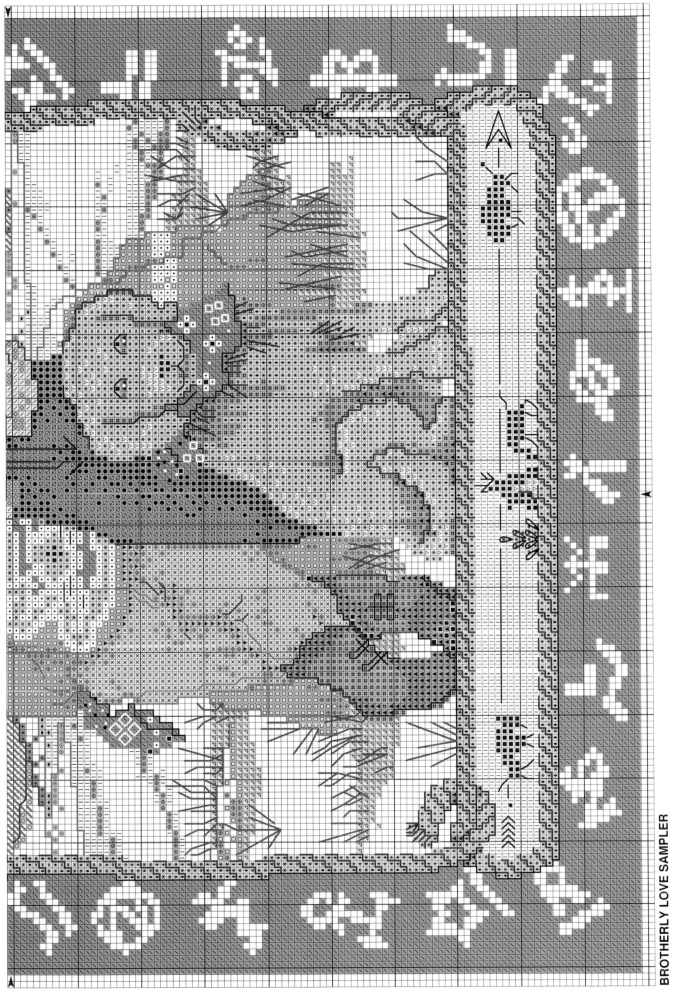

BROTHERLY LOVE SAMPLER

BROTHERLY LOVE SAMPLER

ANCHOR	DMC	
002	000	White
352	300	Deep mahogany
1049	301	Medium mahogany
403	310	Black
9046	321	Christmas red
253	472	Avocado
877	502	Medium blue green
1038	519	Dark sky blue
1041	535	Ash gray
158	747	Light sky blue
1021	761	Salmon
1016	778	Antique mauve
309	781	Topaz
307	783	Christmas gold
178	791	Deep cornflower blue
177	792	Dark cornflower blue
1010	951	Ivory
844	3012	Medium khaki
842	3013	Light khaki
903	3032	Medium mocha
391	3033	Pale mocha
871	3041	Antique violet
875	3813	Light blue green
874	3822	Straw
386	3823	Yellow

HALF CROSS-STITCH (stitch in direction of symbol)

ANCHOR	DMC	
1016	778	Antique mauve

ANCHOR	DMC	
BACKSTITCH		
002	000	White–kerchiefs
352	300	Deep mahogany–lettering, rope, dog, big boy's mouth, eyebrows, hair, boots
403	310	Black–rope, kerchief, buffalo panel, little boy's sweater
9046	321	Christmas red–little boy's shirt, teepee
877	502	Medium blue green–little boy's pants
1041	535	Ash gray–blue jacket, green pants, mid and far hills
844	3012	Medium khaki–mid hills
903	3032	Medium mocha–blonde hair, flesh, little boy's sweater, rocks
871	3041	Antique violet–far hills
STRAIGHT STITCH		
352	300	Deep mahogany–dog hair, rope ends
403	310	Black–buffalo panel
267	470	Medium avocado–grass
307	783	Christmas gold–boys' eyebrows
LAZY DAISY		
403	310	Black–campfire
FRENCH KNOT		
002	000	White–kerchiefs, dog's eyes
403	310	Black–kerchiefs, boys' eyes

Stitch count: 199 high x 151 wide
Finished design sizes:
14-count fabric – 14¼ x 10⅞ inches
11-count fabric – 18⅛ x 13¾ inches
18-count fabric – 11⅛ x 8⅜ inches

---

chart and the center of the fabric. Begin stitching there.

Work cross-stitches using three plies of floss. Use two plies of floss to work the backstitches, straight stitches, lazy daisy stitches, and French knots.

Press finished stitchery on wrong side with a warm iron.

Frame and mat as desired.

PHOTO FRAME

A cross-stitched rope frames a photo (shown on page 81). *Use this chart on 11-count fabric for a vertical version of the album cover.* Finished size is 9×7 inches.

MATERIALS

FABRIC
15×13-inch piece of 14-count blue Aida cloth

THREADS
Cotton embroidery floss in colors listed in the key on page 87

SUPPLIES
Needle; embroidery hoop
1 yard of ¼-inch-wide red decorative trim
½ yard of ⅛-inch-diameter black cording
Kit for 9×7-inch covered frame
Crafts glue

INSTRUCTIONS

Tape or zigzag edges of fabric to prevent fraying. Begin stitching at one corner, 3 inches from the edge of fabric.

Work cross-stitches using three plies of floss. Use two plies to work backstitches and straight stitches.

Follow manufacturer's directions to cover frame. Glue cording around opening in frame. Glue trim around outside edge.

BROTHERLY LOVE SAMPLER

Two boys and a dog conjure up images of the pleasant days of youth when imagination reigned (shown on page 80). Finished design is 14¼×10⅞ inches.

MATERIALS

FABRIC
20×17-inch piece of 14-count white Aida cloth

THREADS
Cotton embroidery floss in colors listed in the key above
Six additional skeins of DMC 321
Three additional skeins of DMC 783
Two additional skeins of DMC 3823
One additional skein of DMC 300 and 781

SUPPLIES
Needle; embroidery hoop
Frame and mat of choice

INSTRUCTIONS

Tape or zigzag edges of fabric to prevent fraying. Find the center of

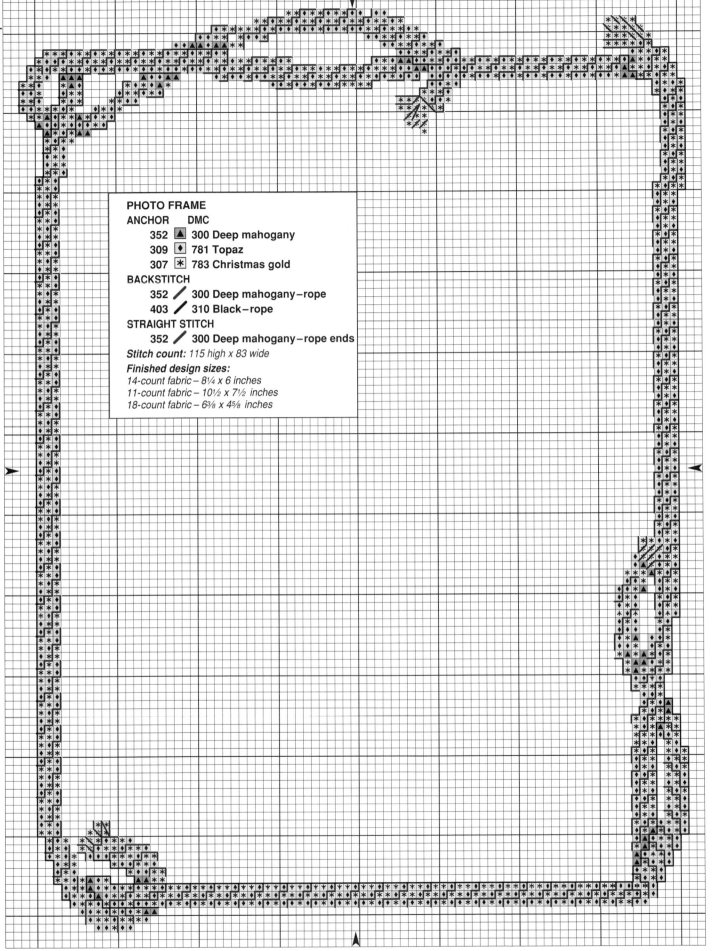

PHOTO FRAME

ANCHOR   DMC

352 ▲ 300 Deep mahogany

309 ♦ 781 Topaz

307 ✳ 783 Christmas gold

BACKSTITCH

352 ╱ 300 Deep mahogany–rope

403 ╱ 310 Black–rope

STRAIGHT STITCH

352 ╱ 300 Deep mahogany–rope ends

Stitch count: 115 high x 83 wide

Finished design sizes:

14-count fabric – 8¼ x 6 inches

11-count fabric – 10½ x 7½ inches

18-count fabric – 6⅜ x 4⅝ inches

DOG

ALBUM COVER

ALBUM COVER		
ANCHOR		**DMC**
002	▫	000 White
352	▲	300 Deep mahogany
1049	⊞	301 Medium mahogany
403	■	310 Black
9046	▨	321 Christmas red
309	◆	781 Topaz
307	✳	783 Christmas gold
874	▽	3822 Straw
386	▯	3823 Yellow

ANCHOR		DMC
BACKSTITCH		
002	╱	000 White – kerchief
352	╱	300 Deep mahogany – rope, dog
403	╱	310 Black – rope, kerchief, buffalo panel, lettering
STRAIGHT STITCH		
352	╱	300 Deep mahogany – dog hair, rope ends
403	╱	310 Black – buffalo panel

ANCHOR		DMC
LAZY DAISY		
403	ᴗ	310 Black – campfire
FRENCH KNOT		
002	○	000 White – kerchief, dog's eyes
403	●	310 Black – kerchief

Stitch count: 98 high x 147 wide

Finished design sizes:
11-count fabric – 8⅞ x 13⅜ inches
14-count fabric – 7 x 10½ inches
18-count fabric – 5⅜ x 8¼ inches

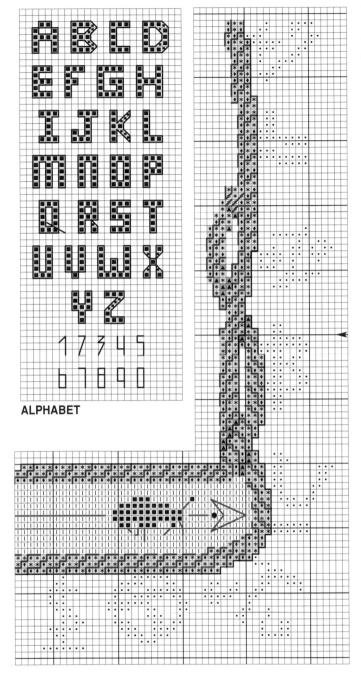

ALPHABET

ALBUM COVER

Stitch a cover for a special collection of photos or a scrapbook of keepsakes (shown on page 82). *Use the photo frame chart on page 87 to make a vertical version.*

Finished size of front cover of album shown is 9×13½ inches.

See information in Instructions for covering other sizes.

MATERIALS

FABRICS

26×20-inch piece of 11-count red Aida cloth (or piece 6 inches higher and 6 inches wider than the size of the album laid open flat)

10×12-inch piece of 14-count beige Aida cloth

¾ yard fabric of choice for lining

Quilt batting

THREADS

Cotton embroidery floss in colors listed in the key on page 88

SUPPLIES

Needle; embroidery hoop; graph paper

2 yards ⅛-inch cording (or 1 inch more than outside measurement of album when laid open flat)

Water-based sealer for needlework finishing

Crafts glue

INSTRUCTIONS

Tape or zigzag edges of fabric to prevent fraying. To help center the design, begin by basting a line around the 11-count Aida cloth, marking the exact size of the album when it is open and laid flat.

Work cross-stitches for album cover on 11-count Aida cloth using four plies of floss. Use two plies of floss to work the backstitches, straight stitches, lazy daisy stitches, and French knots.

Turn chart 180 degrees if you choose to stitch the back cover.

Work cross-stitches for dog on 14-count Aida cloth using three plies of floss. Use two plies to work the backstitches and French knots.

Chart names or other message using graph paper and alphabet provided on page 89, leaving three spaces between letters.

Work cross-stitches for lettering on 14-count Aida cloth using three plies of floss over two threads of the Aida cloth. Outline each letter using two plies of floss over two threads of the Aida cloth.

Press finished stitchery on wrong side with a warm iron.

Apply needlework sealer around outside edges of dog and names according to manufacturer's directions. When completely dry, trim pieces one thread beyond the stitching.

Measure the height and width of the album cover when the book is open flat. Add ½ inch all around for seam allowances. Trim cross-stitched Aida cloth to these dimensions. (Or, trim ½ inch outside the basting line used for placement.) Cut one piece of lining and a piece of quilt batting to this size. Curve the edges of the fabric, batting, and lining if the edges of the album are curved.

Cut two flaps from lining fabric to fit over inside edges of front and back covers. Measure top-to-bottom length of album, adding ½-inch seam allowances. Make flaps approximately 6 inches wide. Stitch a narrow hem on inside edge of each flap.

Lay the batting on a flat surface; top with album cover fabric piece, right side up. Hand-baste the cording around the cover. Lay the flap fabric pieces in place at each end with right sides of fabrics together. Machine-stitch through all layers. Clip curves.

Hand-stitch the lining in place on back side of the batting, turning top and bottom of fabric inward to conceal the raw edges. Turn the album cover right side out and fit over the album.

COWBOY HATBAND

The buffalo roam on this rope-edged band for a cowboy hat (shown on page 83).
Finished band is 1½×9¼ inches.

MATERIALS
FABRIC
6×12-inch piece of 14-count beige Aida cloth
THREADS
Cotton embroidery floss in colors listed in the key below
SUPPLIES
Needle; embroidery hoop
Water-based sealer for needlework finishing

INSTRUCTIONS
Tape or zigzag edges of the fabric to prevent fraying. Find the center of the chart and the center of the fabric. Begin stitching there.

COWBOY HATBAND		
ANCHOR	DMC	
352	300	Deep mahogany
403	310	Black
309	781	Topaz
307	783	Christmas gold
874	3822	Straw
BACKSTITCH		
352	300	Deep mahogany – rope
403	310	Black – buffalos, arrow, outline
403	321	Christmas red – teepee
STRAIGHT STITCH		
352	300	Deep mahogany – rope ends
FRENCH KNOT		
403	310	Black – arrow motif
LAZY DAISY		
403	310	Black – campfire

Stitch count: 24 high x 125 wide
Finished design sizes:
14-count fabric – 1¾ x 9 inches
11-count fabric – 2¼ x 11⅜ inches
18-count fabric – 1⅓ x 7 inches

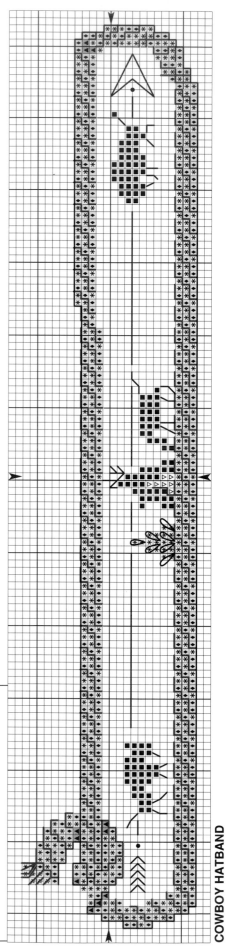

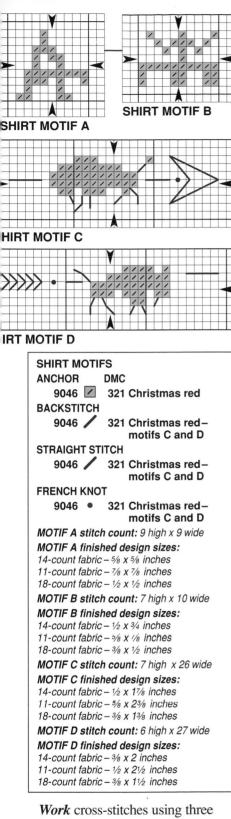

SHIRT MOTIF A

SHIRT MOTIF B

HIRT MOTIF C

IRT MOTIF D

SHIRT MOTIFS

ANCHOR   DMC
9046 ☑   321 Christmas red
BACKSTITCH
9046 ╱   321 Christmas red–
            motifs C and D
STRAIGHT STITCH
9046 ╱   321 Christmas red–
            motifs C and D
FRENCH KNOT
9046 ●   321 Christmas red–
            motifs C and D

MOTIF A stitch count: 9 high x 9 wide
MOTIF A finished design sizes:
14-count fabric – ⅝ x ⅝ inches
11-count fabric – ⅞ x ⅞ inches
18-count fabric – ½ x ½ inches

MOTIF B stitch count: 7 high x 10 wide
MOTIF B finished design sizes:
14-count fabric – ½ x ¾ inches
11-count fabric – ⅝ x ⅞ inches
18-count fabric – ⅜ x ½ inches

MOTIF C stitch count: 7 high x 26 wide
MOTIF C finished design sizes:
14-count fabric – ½ x 1⅞ inches
11-count fabric – ⅝ x 2⅜ inches
18-count fabric – ⅜ x 1⅜ inches

MOTIF D stitch count: 6 high x 27 wide
MOTIF D finished design sizes:
14-count fabric – ⅜ x 2 inches
11-count fabric – ½ x 2½ inches
18-count fabric – ⅜ x 1½ inches

Work cross-stitches using three plies of floss. Use two plies of floss to work backstitches, straight stitches, lazy daisy stitches, and French knots.

Press finished stitchery on wrong side with a warm iron.

Apply needlework sealer around outside edges of stitchery according

Breit Ideas

Go West to find stitching freedom. The motifs within this design provide wide-open opportunities.

✦ Rope borders and cattle brands can turn a child's room into a dude ranch. Window treatments and pillows are easily adapted from the charts in this chapter.

✦ Go beyond the kid stuff and use these cattle brands for napkins for your summer barbecue. Serve up your steaks on rope-bordered place mats decked with cowboy handkerchief napkins.

✦ Save a place for your favorite reader of Westerns by using the bottom border (with the rope and buffalo) for a Texas-size bookmark. Make it any length by selecting your favorite part and enclosing it with the border ends. Glue your stitchery to a piece of leather.

✦ Dog lovers will adore this friendly pooch. Stitch the pup centered on 14-count Aida cloth and surround the canine portrait with the rope border charted on page 87.

✦ Stitch the "be kindly affectioned" motto for your office.

to manufacturer's directions. When completely dry, trim piece one thread beyond stitching. Tack the hatband to the hat.

SHIRT

It takes only a few stitches to make this shirt special (shown on page 83).

MATERIALS
FABRIC
2×2-inch pieces of 14-count waste canvas (four pieces used on the shirt shown)
THREADS
Cotton embroidery floss in color listed in the key above

SUPPLIES
Needle
Shirt or other garment of choice

INSTRUCTIONS
Baste pieces of waste canvas to collar points and pockets of a garment. Find the center of selected motif and the center of the collar or pocket. Begin stitching there.

Work cross-stitches using two plies of floss. Use two plies of floss to work the backstitches, straight stitches, and French knots.

Trim excess canvas from around the stitched motif. Follow manufacturer's instructions to wet and remove canvas threads.

Press finished stitchery on wrong side with a warm iron.

SWEET HOME

Click your ruby slippers together and create some magic with your handiwork. Mary Engelbreit's nostalgic note card art, with its many applications for home decorating, is a perfect way to show the place your home holds in your heart.

all attention to the page in that favorite book you want to remember forever. Focus the spotlight on a favorite photo or a printed announcement. The unique Mary Engelbreit border, re-created in stitchery, above, provides the special treatment.

The symbolic cottage has been remodeled by Mary Engelbreit into a new classic. Stitch this keepsake framed piece, opposite, as a do-it-yourself home improvement project.

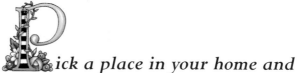

ick a place in your home and
turn it into a cozy corner. *A ruffled pillow,* **above,** *showcases your stitches on*
linen and issues the invitation to make yourself comfortable.

Prompt the compliments on your kitchen wizardry by reminding
one and all that "there's no place like home." Ready-to-stitch products, such
as the towel, apron, and pot holder, **opposite,** *make projects quick and easy.*

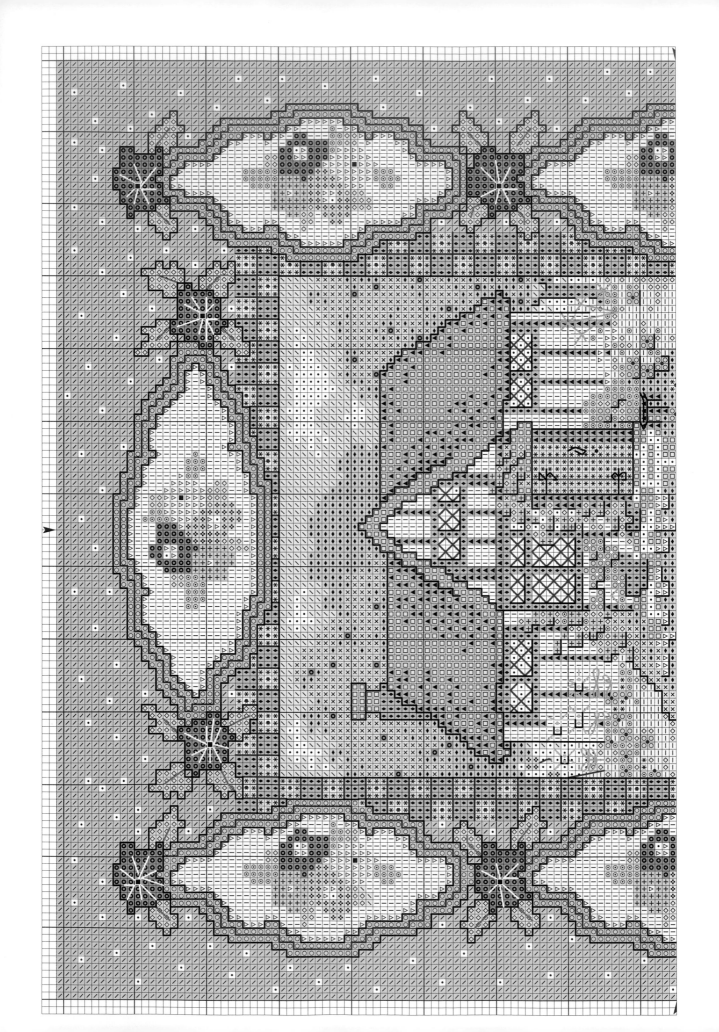

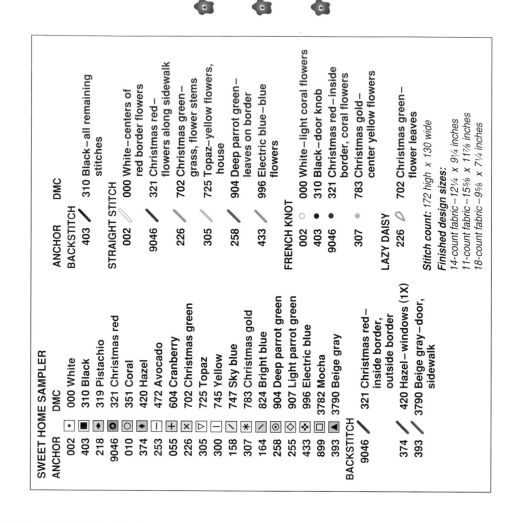

SWEET HOME SAMPLER

ANCHOR	DMC	
002	000	White
403	310	Black
218	319	Pistachio
9046	321	Christmas red
010	351	Coral
374	420	Hazel
253	472	Avocado
055	604	Cranberry
226	702	Christmas green
305	725	Topaz
300	745	Yellow
158	747	Sky blue
307	783	Christmas gold
164	824	Bright blue
258	904	Deep parrot green
255	907	Light parrot green
433	996	Electric blue
899	3782	Mocha
393	3790	Beige gray

BACKSTITCH

ANCHOR	DMC	
9046	321	Christmas red – inside border, outside border
374	420	Hazel – windows (1X)
393	3790	Beige gray – door, sidewalk
403	310	Black – all remaining stitches

STRAIGHT STITCH

ANCHOR	DMC	
002	000	White – centers of red border flowers
9046	321	Christmas red – flowers along sidewalk
226	702	Christmas green – grass, flower stems
305	725	Topaz – yellow flowers, house
258	904	Deep parrot green – leaves on border
433	996	Electric blue – blue flowers

FRENCH KNOT

ANCHOR	DMC	
002	000	White – light coral flowers
403	310	Black – door knob
9046	321	Christmas red – inside border, coral flowers
307	783	Christmas gold – center yellow flowers

LAZY DAISY

ANCHOR	DMC	
226	702	Christmas green – flower leaves

Stitch count: 172 high x 130 wide
Finished design sizes:
14-count fabric – 12¼ x 9¼ inches
11-count fabric – 15⅝ x 11⅞ inches
18-count fabric – 9⅝ x 7¼ inches

SWEET HOME SAMPLER

This new classic makes a happy statement about your home and its comforts (shown on page 95). Finished design is 12¼×9¼ inches.

MATERIALS
FABRIC
18×15-inch piece of 14-count white Aida cloth
THREADS
Cotton embroidery floss in colors listed in the key above
Four additional skeins of DMC 824
One additional skein of DMC 310, 351, 725, 745, 907, and white

SUPPLIES
Needle; embroidery hoop
Frame and mat of choice

INSTRUCTIONS
Tape or zigzag edges of Aida cloth to prevent fraying. Find the center of the chart and the fabric. Begin stitching there.

Work cross-stitches using three plies of floss. Use two plies to work the backstitches, straight stitches, lazy daisy stitches, and French knots.

Press finished stitchery on wrong side with a warm iron.

Frame and mat as desired.

BOOKMARK

Too pretty to hide, this bookmark (shown on page 94) *belongs on display with your favorite book.* Finished size is 8×2½ inches, not including tassel.

MATERIALS
FABRICS
7×3-inch piece of 14-count cream perforated paper
9×3-inch piece of felted imitation suede fabric
THREADS
Cotton embroidery floss in colors listed in the key on page 101
SUPPLIES
Needle; pinking scissors
Tacky crafts glue
3-inch tassel of choice

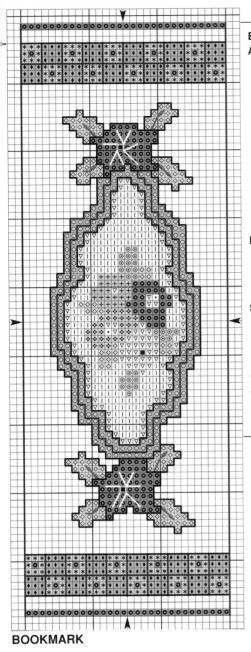

BOOKMARK

ANCHOR		DMC
002	⊡	000 White
403	■	310 Black
9046	⊙	321 Christmas red
010	○	351 Coral
374	◆	420 Hazel
055	✛	604 Cranberry
305	▽	725 Topaz
300	ꟷ	745 Yellow
307	✳	783 Christmas gold
258	◉	904 Deep parrot green
255	◈	907 Light parrot green
433	✿	996 Electric blue

BACKSTITCH

9046	╱	321 Christmas red–borders and center motif
403	╱	310 Black–all remaining stitches

STRAIGHT STITCH

002	╱	000 White–centers of red flowers
258	╱	904 Deep parrot green–leaves

Stitch count: 87 high x 30 wide
Finished design sizes:
14-count fabric – 6¼ x 2⅛ inches
11-count fabric – 7⅞ x 2¾ inches
18-count fabric – 4⅞ x 1⅝ inches

BOOKMARK

INSTRUCTIONS

Find the center of the chart and the center of the perforated paper. Begin stitching there.

Work cross-stitches using two plies of floss over one square of the perforated paper. Use two plies of floss to work the backstitches; use three plies to work straight stitches. Trim perforated paper one row beyond stitched edge.

Cut an 8×2½-inch piece of the suede fabric with pinking scissors. Fold and turn back corners of one end of fabric, forming a pointed end. Glue corners in place.

Center cross-stitched perforated paper on suede fabric, ⅛ inch from top and sides. Use a small amount of glue under stitched areas to hold in place.

Glue loop on tassel to back of suede fabric at point on the bottom.

PICTURE-FRAME MAT

Border a favorite quote or keepsake with this cheerful stitchery (shown on page 94).

Finished mat is 9¼×7 inches with a 6×3¾-inch opening. To increase the outer dimensions, add rows of blue cross-stitches sprinkled with white cross-stitches.

MATERIALS

FABRICS

16×14-inch piece of 18-count white Aida cloth

10¼×8-inch piece of fleece

THREADS

Cotton embroidery floss in colors listed in the key on page 103

One additional skein of DMC 824

SUPPLIES

Needle; embroidery hoop

9¼×7-inch piece of mat board with a 6×3¾-inch rectangular opening

Tacky crafts glue

Frame of choice

INSTRUCTIONS

Tape or zigzag edges of Aida cloth to prevent fraying.

Use the picture-frame chart on pages 102 and 103.

Begin stitching at a corner of the pattern, 3 inches from edges of the Aida cloth.

Work cross-stitches using two plies of floss. Use two plies of floss to work the straight stitches and French knots. Use one ply of floss to work backstitches.

Press finished stitchery on wrong side with a warm iron.

Place fleece on top of the mat board. Glue raw edges (½-inch allowance) to back of mat.

Cut the mat opening from the fleece diagonally from corner to corner, making an X cut. Trim the excess fleece from points on the X.

Stretch raw edges slightly and glue to back of mat board.

Trim cross-stitched Aida cloth, leaving ½-inch edge beyond the stitching. Place stitching on top of fleece. Glue the edges to the back of the mat board, mitering the corners.

Cut, trim, and glue center opening, following directions as for the fleece.

Use the finished mat with frame of choice.

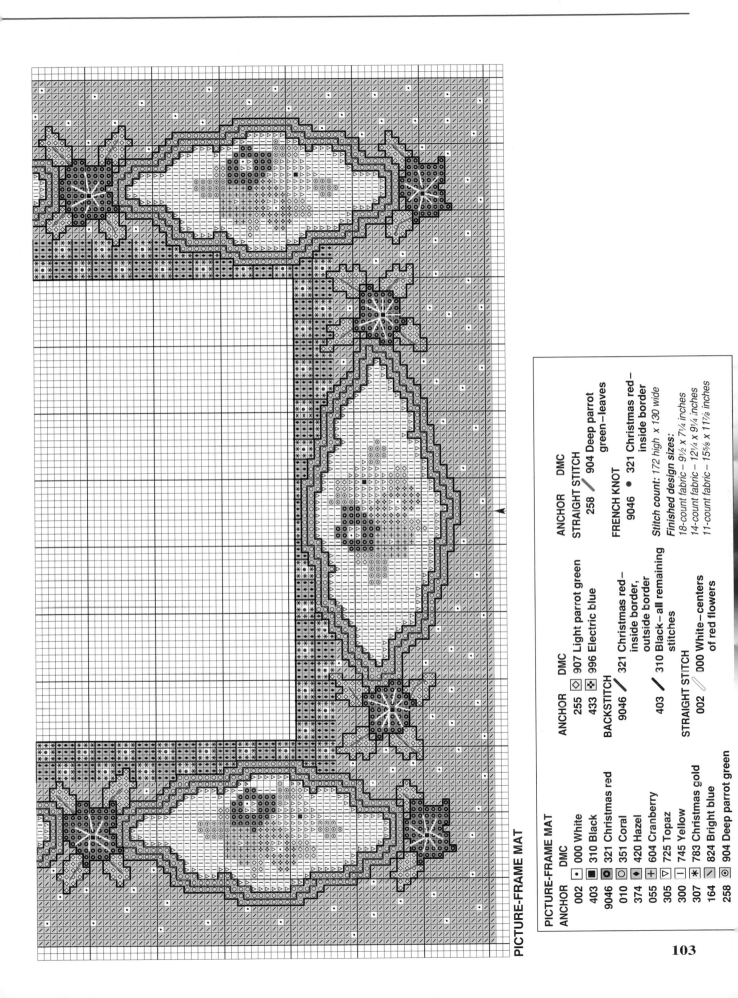

PICTURE-FRAME MAT

ANCHOR		DMC	
002	•	000	White
403	■	310	Black
9046	◉	321	Christmas red
010	○	351	Coral
374	◆	420	Hazel
055	+	604	Cranberry
305	▽	725	Topaz
300	—	745	Yellow
307	✱	783	Christmas gold
164	/	824	Bright blue
258	◉	904	Deep parrot green

ANCHOR		DMC	
255	◇	907	Light parrot green
433	✚	996	Electric blue

BACKSTITCH
9046 / 321 Christmas red—inside border, outside border
403 / 310 Black—all remaining stitches

STRAIGHT STITCH
002 / 000 White—centers of red flowers

ANCHOR	DMC

STRAIGHT STITCH
258 / 904 Deep parrot green—leaves

FRENCH KNOT
9046 • 321 Christmas red—inside border

Stitch count: 172 high x 130 wide

Finished design sizes:
18-count fabric — 9½ x 7¼ inches
14-count fabric — 12¼ x 9¼ inches
11-count fabric — 15⅝ x 11⅞ inches

PICTURE-FRAME MAT

COTTAGE PILLOW

COTTAGE PILLOW

ANCHOR		DMC	
002	·	000	White
218	◆	319	Pistachio
9046	◉	321	Christmas red
010	○	351	Coral
374	◆	420	Hazel
253	−	472	Avocado
055	+	604	Cranberry
226	×	702	Christmas green
305	▽	725	Topaz
300	⊡	745	Yellow
158	⁄	747	Sky blue
307	✳	783	Christmas gold
258	◉	904	Deep parrot green
255	◇	907	Light parrot green
433	✤	996	Electric blue
899	▢	3782	Mocha
393	▲	3790	Beige gray

BACKSTITCH

9046	⁄	321	Christmas red– border
374	⁄	420	Hazel–windows, sidewalk
393	⁄	3790	Beige gray–doors
403	⁄	310	Black–all remaining stitches

ANCHOR		DMC	
STRAIGHT STITCH			
9046	⁄	321	Christmas red– flowers on sidewalk
226	⁄	702	Christmas green– grass, flower stems
305	⁄	725	Topaz–yellow flowers, house
433	⁄	996	Electric blue–blue flowers, house

FRENCH KNOT

002	○	000	White–flowers under window
9046	●	321	Christmas red– border, coral flowers
307	●	783	Christmas gold– center yellow flowers
403	●	310	Black–door knob

LAZY DAISY

226	⟋	702	Christmas green– flower leaves

Stitch count: 81 high x 81 wide

Finished design sizes:
28-count fabric – 5¾ x 5¾ inches
22 count fabric – 7⅜ x 7⅜ inches
36-count fabric – 4½ x 4½ inches

COTTAGE PILLOW

An invitation to get comfortable, this pillow (shown on page 96) *is sitting pretty no matter where you place it.*

Finished size is 18 inches square, including ruffle.

MATERIALS

FABRICS

18×18-inch piece of 28-count buttercup Meran cloth

14×14-inch piece of fleece for underlining

1½ yards moiré taffeta or fabric of choice for ruffle, backing, and piping

THREADS

Cotton embroidery floss in colors listed in the key above

Two additional skeins of DMC 420

One additional skein of DMC 321 and 783

SUPPLIES

Needle; embroidery hoop

1½ yards of ⅛-inch cording

14-inch pillow form or polyester fiberfill

INSTRUCTIONS

Tape or zigzag edges of Meran cloth to prevent fraying. Find the center of the chart and the center of the fabric. Begin stitching there.

Work cross-stitches using three plies of floss over two threads of the Meran cloth. Use two plies of floss to work the backstitches, lazy daisy stitches, straight stitches, and French knots.

Count 72 threads (36 stitches) out from inner border to repeat the 6-stitch-wide border.

Press finished stitchery on wrong side with a warm iron. Trim fabric 1 inch beyond outer border.

Place the 14-inch square of fleece on the back of cross-stitched piece, basting along outside edge.

Quilt, by hand or machine, around center motif and both sides of the outer border.

Cut a 14-inch square from taffeta for pillow back. Cut a 1¼×55-inch piping strip, piecing if necessary. For ruffle, cut 6-inch ruffle strips, piecing as needed to make a total of 105 inches.

Sew short ends of piping strips together to form a continuous circle. Center cording lengthwise on the wrong side of the taffeta piping strip with the ends of the cording touching. Fold fabric around cording with raw edges together. Use a zipper foot to sew through both fabric layers close to cording. Pin cording to pillow front with raw edges even. Stitch in place.

Sew the ruffle strips together to form a circle. Fold strips, wrong sides together, and press fold line. Sew a gathering thread through both layers of ruffle, ½ inch from raw edges. Pull threads to fit perimeter of pillow front with raw edges even; adjust gathers evenly. Sew ruffle to pillow along stitching line of piping.

Sew pillow front to back, with right sides facing, keeping ruffle tucked inside. Leave an opening for turning. Clip corners, turn right side out, and press.

Insert pillow form or stuff firmly. Slip-stitch the opening closed.

APRON

APRON

Meal-making becomes merry when the cook wears this message (shown on page 97).
Finished insert is 8⅛×5½ inches.

MATERIALS
FABRIC
14×11-inch piece of 14-count Rustico cloth
THREADS
Cotton embroidery floss in colors listed in the key below
SUPPLIES
Needle; embroidery hoop
Apron pattern of choice with fabric and sewing supplies as required

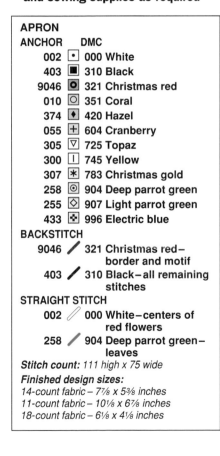

APRON		
ANCHOR		DMC
002	·	000 White
403	■	310 Black
9046	◉	321 Christmas red
010	○	351 Coral
374	◆	420 Hazel
055	+	604 Cranberry
305	▽	725 Topaz
300	❙	745 Yellow
307	✳	783 Christmas gold
258	◉	904 Deep parrot green
255	◇	907 Light parrot green
433	✦	996 Electric blue
BACKSTITCH		
9046	╱	321 Christmas red– border and motif
403	╱	310 Black–all remaining stitches
STRAIGHT STITCH		
002	╱╱	000 White–centers of red flowers
258	╱	904 Deep parrot green– leaves

Stitch count: 111 high x 75 wide
Finished design sizes:
14-count fabric – 7⅞ x 5⅜ inches
11-count fabric – 10⅛ x 6⅞ inches
18-count fabric – 6⅛ x 4⅛ inches

INSTRUCTIONS

Tape or zigzag edges of fabric to prevent fraying. Find the center of the chart and the center of the fabric. Begin stitching there.

Work cross-stitches using three plies of floss over one thread of Rustico cloth. Use two plies to work backstitches and straight stitches.

Press finished stitchery on wrong side with a warm iron.

Set cross-stitched insert into apron bib, trimming as needed and allowing for seam allowance.

Complete apron with additional trim as desired.

POT HOLDER

Use this cross-stitched reminder to collect appreciation when you serve a dish hot from the oven (shown on page 97).
Finished size is a 7¾-inch square pot holder.

MATERIALS
FABRIC
Ecru quilted terry-cloth prefinished pot holder with insert of 14-count ecru Aida cloth
THREADS
Cotton embroidery floss in colors listed in the key on page 108
SUPPLIES
Needle

INSTRUCTIONS

Find the center of the chart and the center of the Aida cloth insert. Begin stitching there.

Work cross-stitches using three plies of floss. Use two plies of floss to work the backstitches and straight stitches.

HAND TOWEL

Stitch a light variation of the border pattern by omitting the solid blue stitching and sprinkling blue stitches in place of the white ones (shown on page 97).
Finished border is 3×14 inches.

MATERIALS
FABRIC
Ecru terry-cloth towel with a 3×14-inch insert of 14-count Aida cloth
THREADS
Cotton embroidery floss in colors listed in the key on page 109
SUPPLIES
Needle; embroidery hoop

INSTRUCTIONS

Find the center of the hand towel chart on pages 108 and 109 and the center of the towel insert. Begin stitching there.

Work cross-stitches using three plies of floss. Use two plies of floss to work the backstitches, straight stitches, and French knots.

Press finished stitchery on wrong side with a warm iron.

POT HOLDER

ANCHOR		DMC	
403	■	310	Black
9046	◉	321	Christmas red
374	◆	420	Hazel
307	✳	783	Christmas gold
255	◇	907	Light parrot green

ANCHOR		DMC	
BACKSTITCH			
9046	╱	321	Christmas red—border
403	╱	310	Black—all remaining stitches
STRAIGHT STITCH			
002	╱	000	White—center of flower
258	╱	904	Deep parrot green—leaves

Stitch count: *57 high x 93 wide*
Finished design sizes:
14-count fabric – 4 x 6⅝ inches
11-count fabric – 5⅛ x 8½ inches
18-count fabric – 3⅛ x 5⅛ inches

HAND TOWEL

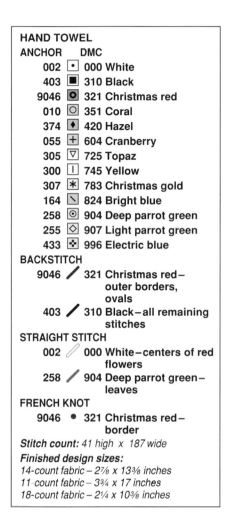

HAND TOWEL

ANCHOR		DMC	
002	⊡	000	White
403	■	310	Black
9046	◉	321	Christmas red
010	○	351	Coral
374	◆	420	Hazel
055	⊞	604	Cranberry
305	▽	725	Topaz
300	⌶	745	Yellow
307	✳	783	Christmas gold
164	◩	824	Bright blue
258	◉	904	Deep parrot green
255	◇	907	Light parrot green
433	✛	996	Electric blue

BACKSTITCH

9046	╱	321	Christmas red– outer borders, ovals
403	╱	310	Black–all remaining stitches

STRAIGHT STITCH

002	╱	000	White–centers of red flowers
258	╱	904	Deep parrot green– leaves

FRENCH KNOT

9046	●	321	Christmas red– border

Stitch count: 41 high x 187 wide

Finished design sizes:
14-count fabric – 2⅞ x 13⅜ inches
11-count fabric – 3¾ x 17 inches
18-count fabric – 2¼ x 10⅜ inches

Breit Ideas

Decorating applications abound in this homey design.

✿ Table linens are a perfect place for stitched excerpts from the border design. Use the bookmark chart to stitch a single motif and the towel border to decorate a table runner or place mat. In a corner of a napkin, stitch the red flower with its four leaves or the group of four flowers from the center of the lozenge.

✿ Color your own flowers to match your tableware. It's easy to substitute floss colors in these one-color blooms.

✿ Do it in beads. Work the bookmark motif in beads and finish it off as a pin or barrette.

✿ A serving tray with a cross-stitched insert of the cottage from the pillow chart calls for tea and scones.

✿ Dress your windows with a valance stitched from the border pattern. Make it fast and dramatic by using 11-count fabric.

✿ College kids or others who have recently left the nest can be reminded cheerfully that "there's no place like home." Stitch it on a sweatshirt, pillow, or treasure box, or frame it.

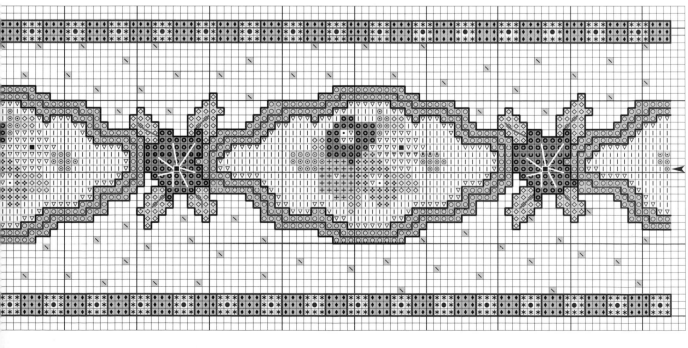

NESTING
PLACE

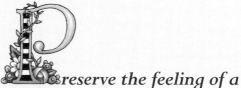

Preserve the feeling of a
perfect late-summer day—the shade of a tree in your backyard and
lazy-day dreaming—in stitchery. Use Mary Engelbreit's message and
cross your stitches with pleasant thoughts.

*olored with autumnal warmth, this sampler, **opposite,** will help you collect your thoughts as you stitch. A boy dreams among the leaves while school and games are forgotten in this richly detailed design.*

*Acorns and oak leaves surround treasures in quick-to-stitch applications, **above.** Make a padded frame or insert your stitchery in a collector's cabinet to highlight your favorite things.*

leasant thoughts should always
be saved. This chamois-backed, cross-stitched book cover, opposite,
personalizes your journal and makes it special.

For safekeeping of your mementos, nothing is more appropriate
than a wooden box adorned with cross-stitched oak leaves and acorns, above.
It makes the perfect home for buttons, buckeyes, love letters, stamps from
far-off places, and ticket stubs.

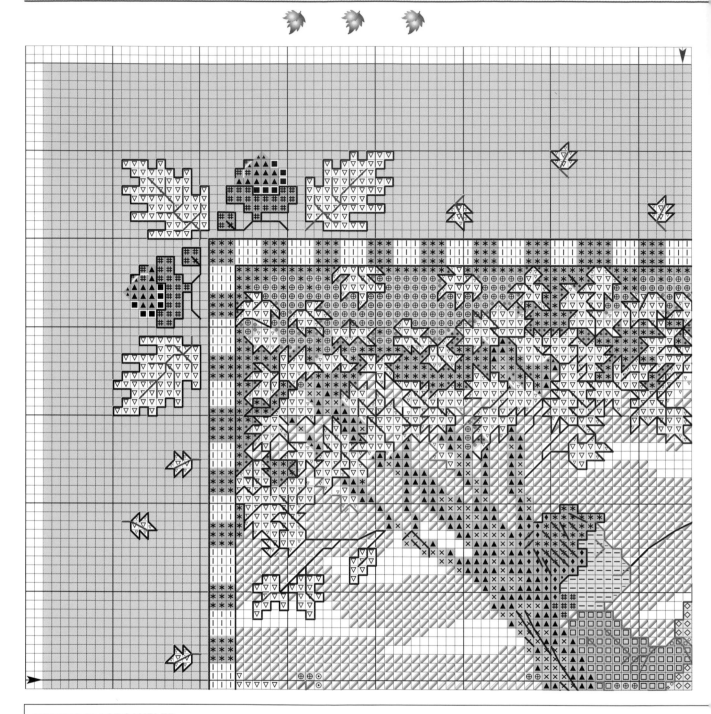

NESTING PLACE SAMPLER

ANCHOR		DMC	
387	·	Ecru	
403	■	310	Black
9046	◉	321	Christmas red
310	⊞	434	Chestnut
162	◆	517	Wedgwood blue
168	✤	597	Light turquoise
167	◇	598	Medium turquoise
324	✳	721	Bittersweet
295	▽	726	Topaz
361	▢	738	Tan
303	⊕	742	Tangerine

ANCHOR		DMC	
301	I	744	Yellow
380	▲	838	Deep beige brown
378	✕	841	True beige brown
256	⊙	906	Parrot green
338	◆	921	Copper
1010	—	951	Ivory
851	◺	3808	Deep turquoise
278	△	3819	Moss green

OPTIONAL CROSS-STITCH

851	▢	3808	Deep turquoise– border

HALF CROSS-STITCH
(stitch in direction of symbol)

ANCHOR		DMC	
361	╱	738	Tan–distant hills
301	╱	744	Yellow–grass, distant hills
378	╱	841	True beige brown– distant hills
256	╱	906	Parrot green–grass
928	╱	3761	Sky blue–sky
278	╱	3819	Moss green–grass, distant hills

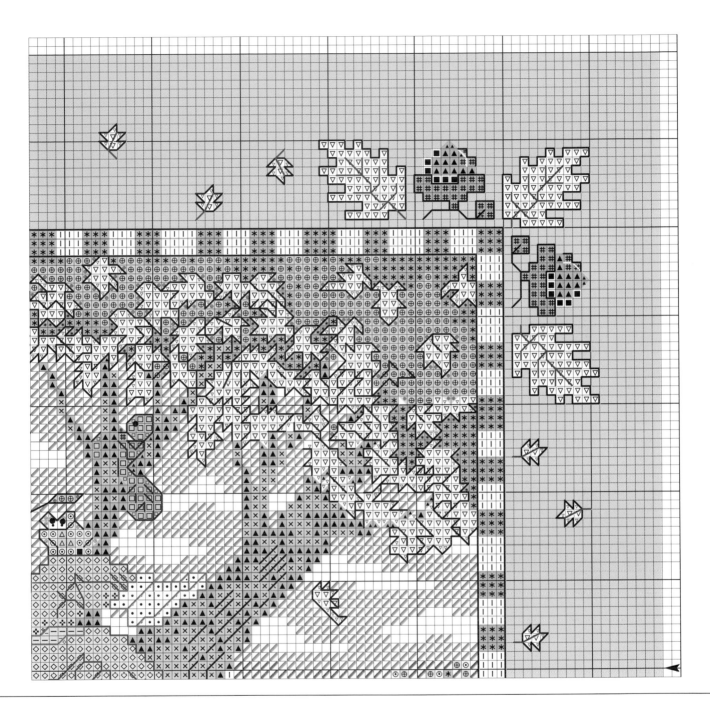

ANCHOR	DMC		ANCHOR	DMC		ANCHOR	DMC	
BACKSTITCH			**BACKSTITCH**			**FRENCH KNOT**		
387		Ecru–acorns, lunchbox	378	841	True beige brown–face, hand, sweater, shoes, books, distant houses, some tree leaves	403	310	Black–frog's eyes
403	310	Black–turtle, frog, ball, apple stem				9046	321	Christmas red–lettering
9046	321	Christmas red–banner, lettering, lunchbox handle, distant houses	338	921	Copper–leaf veins	380	838	Deep beige brown–squirrel's eye
			851	3808	Deep turquoise–distant trees	378	841	True beige brown–turtle's eye
310	434	Chestnut–leaves, leaf veins, frog, squirrel	**STRAIGHT STITCH**					
162	517	Wedgwood blue–book, boy's pants	310	434	Chestnut–boy's hair	*Stitch count: 140 high x 146 wide*		
324	721	Bittersweet–leaf veins, book	324	721	Bittersweet–tall grass	*Finished design sizes:*		
380	838	Deep beige brown–leaves, acorns, pencil, tree, piece of straw, banner	303	742	Tangerine–tall grass	*14-count fabric – 10 x 10⅜ inches*		
			380	838	Deep beige brown–tree bark	*11-count fabric –12¾ x 13¼ inches*		
			851	3808	Deep turquoise–grass	*18-count fabric – 7¾ x 8⅛ inches*		

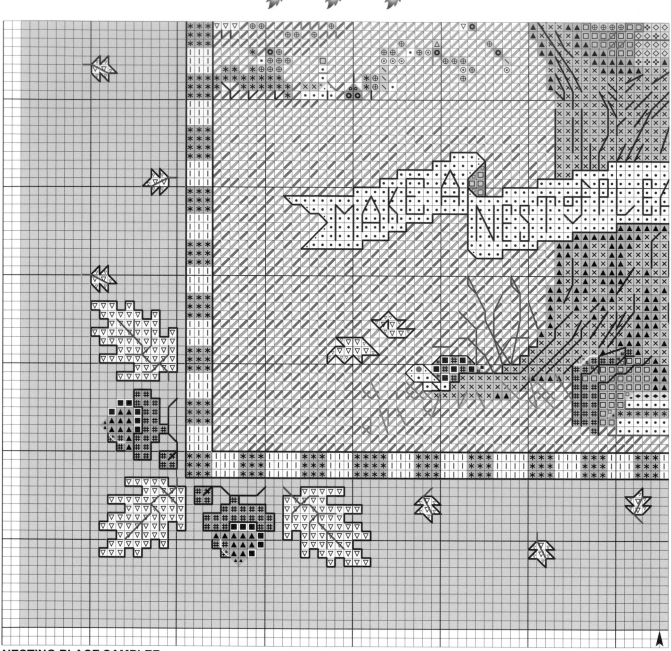

NESTING PLACE SAMPLER

NESTING PLACE SAMPLER

The border was stitched on a separate piece of fabric and made into a mat for added dimension (shown on page 112). Use the optional instructions on page 120 to stitch the design as one piece. Finished design is 10×10⅜ inches.

MATERIALS

FABRICS
16×16-inch piece of 14-count white Aida cloth
16×16-inch piece of 14-count cadet blue Aida cloth

THREADS
Cotton embroidery floss in colors listed in key on pages 116–117
Two additional skeins of DMC 838

One additional skein of DMC ecru, 310, 721, 726, 742, 744, 841, and 3761

SUPPLIES
Needle; embroidery hoop
Black glass seed beads (approximately 200)
12×12-inch piece of fleece
11×11¼-inch piece of mat board
Crafts glue
Frame of choice

INSTRUCTIONS

Tape or zigzag edges of white Aida cloth to prevent fraying. Find the center of the chart and the center of the white Aida cloth. Begin stitching there.

Work cross-stitches and half cross-stitches using three plies of floss. Use two plies of floss to work the straight stitches, backstitches, and French knots.

End stitching on the white Aida cloth by backstitching the outside line around checkerboard design.

Tape or zigzag edges of cadet blue Aida cloth to prevent fraying. Begin stitching checkerboard border at one corner, approximately 4 inches from edges of fabric.

Work cross-stitches using three plies of floss. Use two plies of floss to work the backstitches. Add glass

seed beads randomly, using photo on page 112 as a guide.

Center fleece on back of stitched cadet blue Aida cloth and baste or stitch a line just inside the checkerboard center. Trim Aida cloth to 13×13¼ inches with stitched border centered.

Cut a 7×7⅜-inch opening in the center of the mat board. Place the fleece-backed border over the mat board. Cut away the center of the Aida cloth, leaving ½ inch inside the checkerboard border. Clip corners carefully. Glue allowance to back of mat board, carefully aligning the checkerboard border with the opening in the mat board. Complete by gluing outside edges of Aida cloth to back of mat board.

Place blue Aida cloth mat on top of white Aida cloth stitchery and frame as desired.

Optional Instructions

Stitch the border directly on the white Aida cloth, omitting the cadet blue Aida cloth and mat board. Use DMC 3808 to fill the border background with cross-stitches. Sew glass seed beads on top of cross-stitches.

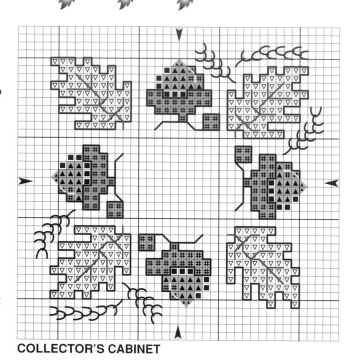

COLLECTOR'S CABINET

COLLECTOR'S CABINET

A nature-inspired wreath of oak leaves and acorns is just enough stitchery to make a miniature collection of treasures special (shown on page 113). Finished insert is 3½×3½ inches.

MATERIALS

FABRIC
6×6-inch piece of 28-count cream Jubilee cloth

THREADS
Cotton embroidery floss in colors listed in the key above right

SUPPLIES
Needle
Embroidery hoop
4½×4½-inch piece of fleece
8¼×9¼-inch small collector's cabinet with 3½×3½-inch opening for an insert
Crafts glue
½ yard of ¼-inch-wide black braid

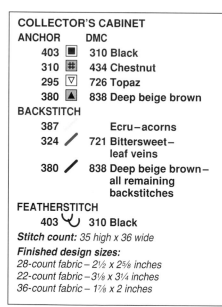

COLLECTOR'S CABINET

ANCHOR		DMC	
403	■	310	Black
310	⊞	434	Chestnut
295	▽	726	Topaz
380	▲	838	Deep beige brown
BACKSTITCH			
387			Ecru – acorns
324	╱	721	Bittersweet – leaf veins
380	╱	838	Deep beige brown – all remaining backstitches
FEATHERSTITCH			
403	↭	310	Black

Stitch count: 35 high x 36 wide
Finished design sizes:
28-count fabric – 2½ x 2⅝ inches
22-count fabric – 3⅛ x 3¼ inches
36-count fabric – 1⅞ x 2 inches

INSTRUCTIONS

Tape or zigzag edges of Jubilee cloth to prevent fraying. Find the center of Jubilee cloth and center of the chart. Begin stitching there.

Work cross-stitches using three plies of floss over two threads of the Jubilee cloth. Use two plies of floss to work the featherstitches and the backstitches.

Trim finished stitchery to 4½×4½ inches with design centered. Back stitchery with fleece. Center fleece-backed stitchery on board for insert provided with the cabinet. Glue edges to the back of the board. Glue black braid around edges of insert. Mount in cabinet following manufacturer's directions.

OAK LEAF FRAME

Easy stitching on 11-count fabric creates a padded showcase for a favorite photograph (shown on page 113). Finished frame is 6½×6½ inches with a 3½×3½-inch opening.

MATERIALS

FABRIC
12×12-inch piece of 11-count pearl Aida cloth

THREADS
Cotton embroidery floss in colors listed in the key on page 121

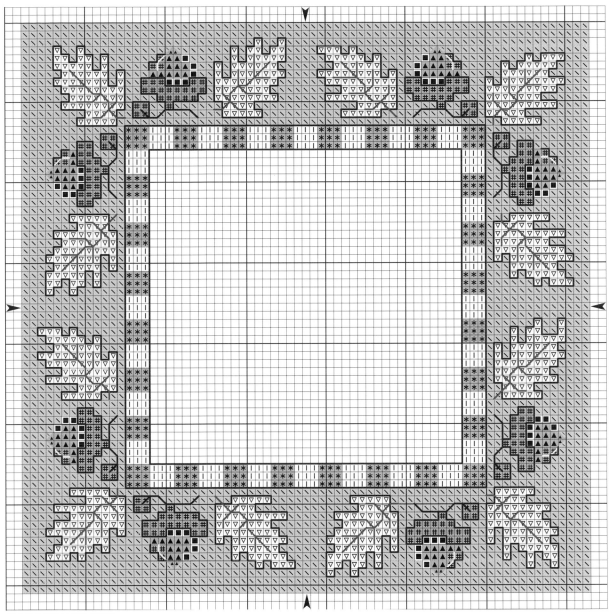

OAK LEAF FRAME

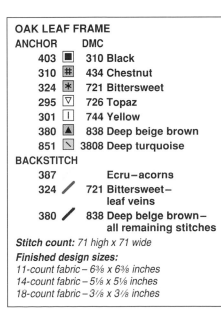

OAK LEAF FRAME

ANCHOR		DMC	
403	■	310	Black
310	#	434	Chestnut
324	*	721	Bittersweet
295	▽	726	Topaz
301			744	Yellow
380	▲	838	Deep beige brown
851	◣	3808	Deep turquoise

BACKSTITCH

387			Ecru–acorns
324	/	721	Bittersweet– leaf veins
380	/	838	Deep beige brown– all remaining stitches

Stitch count: 71 high x 71 wide

Finished design sizes:
11-count fabric – 6⅜ x 6⅜ inches
14-count fabric – 5⅛ x 5⅛ inches
18-count fabric – 3⅞ x 3⅞ inches

SUPPLIES

Needle; embroidery hoop
6½×6½-inch piece of mat board
7½×15-inch piece of fleece
Crafts glue
¾ yard of ½-inch-wide blue flat braid
½ yard of ½-inch-wide gold flat braid
6½×6½-inch piece of foam-core board
Easel back (optional)

INSTRUCTIONS

Tape or zigzag edges of Aida cloth to prevent fraying. Find the center of the Aida cloth and the center of the chart. Count to inner edge of border on one side and begin stitching there.

Work cross-stitches using three plies of floss. Use two plies of floss to work the backstitches.

Cut a 3½×3½-inch opening in the center of the mat board. Cut two 6½×6½-inch pieces of fleece. Glue one piece of fleece to the board, then cut fleece away from the center opening.

Trim stitched Aida cloth to 7½×7½ inches with stitchery centered. Center the second 6½×6½-inch piece of fleece on the back of stitchery.

Place fleece-backed stitchery on top of fleece-covered mat board. Glue the outside edges of the Aida cloth to the back of the mat board, mitering the corners.

Cut window opening in the Aida cloth by making an X cut from corner to corner of the opening in the mat board. Trim excess fabric away, leaving ½ inch on all sides to glue to the back of the mat board.

Glue blue flat braid around the outer edge of the front of the frame. Glue gold flat braid around the inside opening.

Use foam-core board to make a frame back. Glue to three edges of mat board, leaving the top open to insert a picture. Add an easel back to the foam-core board, place the frame on an easel, or hang it on a wall with ribbon.

PLEASANT THOUGHTS BOOK COVER

Slipcover your dreams, poems, or memories with your stitchery. Add texture with some charms and a chamois backing fabric for this journal (shown on page 114). Finished front of book cover is 8½×6¼ inches.

MATERIALS
FABRICS
14×12-inch piece of 27-count blue Linda cloth
12×20-inch chamois
9½×12-inch piece of fabric of choice for backing
THREADS
Cotton embroidery floss in colors listed in the key below right
SUPPLIES
Needle; embroidery hoop
9½×7-inch piece of fleece
1½ yards of ⅛-inch-diameter cord for piping
5 brass charms
8×5½-inch book with ½-inch spine

INSTRUCTIONS
Tape or zigzag edges of Linda cloth to prevent fraying. Find the center of the chart and the center of the cloth. Begin stitching there.

Work cross-stitches using three plies of floss over two threads of Linda cloth. Use two plies to work featherstitches and backstitches.

Measure the book's cover. If different from book specified, adjust the following measurements.

Trim Linda cloth to 9½×7 inches with design centered, and place fleece on the back of the stitchery. Cut a 9½×7½ piece of chamois. Stitch chamois back to left edge of the stitchery with right sides together, using a ½-inch seam.

Cut a 1½×43-inch piece of chamois, piecing as necessary, to make piping. Fold chamois strip in half lengthwise with cord inside. Using a zipper foot, stitch close to cord, leaving ½-inch stitching lip. Stitch piping around all four sides of the book cover.

Cut two 9½×5-inch pieces of chamois for the flaps. With right sides together, place two chamois flaps on top of each end of the book cover, then center backing fabric on top of cover and end flaps. (The backing fabric is not as wide as the cover.)

Stitch around all four sides of the cover, through all thicknesses, using the piping stitching line as a guide. This will leave a raw edge of the backing fabric open. Trim seams and turn cover right side out.

Sew charms around lettering as desired. Slip cover onto book.

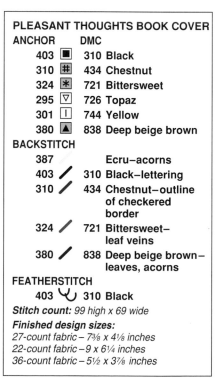

PLEASANT THOUGHTS BOOK COVER		
ANCHOR	DMC	
403 ■	310	Black
310 ⊞	434	Chestnut
324 ✳	721	Bittersweet
295 ▽	726	Topaz
301 ⫿	744	Yellow
380 ▲	838	Deep beige brown
BACKSTITCH		
387		Ecru–acorns
403 ╱	310	Black–lettering
310 ╱	434	Chestnut–outline of checkered border
324 ╱	721	Bittersweet–leaf veins
380 ╱	838	Deep beige brown–leaves, acorns
FEATHERSTITCH		
403 ⋃	310	Black

Stitch count: 99 high x 69 wide
Finished design sizes:
27-count fabric – 7⅜ x 4⅛ inches
22-count fabric – 9 x 6¼ inches
36-count fabric – 5½ x 3⅞ inches

PLEASANT THOUGHTS BOOK COVER

OAK BOX

OAK BOX

ANCHOR		DMC	
403	■	310	Black
310	⊞	434	Chestnut
324	✳	721	Bittersweet
295	▽	726	Topaz
301	⊡	744	Yellow
380	▲	838	Deep beige brown
851	◤	3808	Deep turquoise

BACKSTITCH

387		Ecru – acorns
324	╱	721 Bittersweet – leaf veins
380	╱	838 Deep beige brown – all remaining stitches

FEATHERSTITCH

403	⌣	310 Black

Stitch count: 88 high x 59 wide

Finished design sizes:
14-count fabric – 6¼ x 4¼ inches
11-count fabric – 8 x 5⅜ inches
18-count fabric – 4⅞ x 3¼ inches

OAK BOX

Squirrel away your treasures in an acorn-decorated oak box (shown on page 115).
Finished box is 6½×8½ inches with a 5¼×7¼-inch stitchery insert.

MATERIALS

FABRIC
10×14-inch piece of 14-count Yorkshire green Aida cloth
THREADS
Cotton embroidery floss in colors listed in the key above
SUPPLIES
Needle; embroidery hoop
6¼×8¼-inch piece of fleece
6½×8½-inch rectangular oak box with a 5¼×7¼-inch insert
Crafts glue

Breit Ideas

Autumn flavors Mary Engelbreit's Nesting Place art. The excerpts from the design bring the warm colors inside.

🍂 Use the Collector's Cabinet pattern to make 4-inch quilt blocks. Stitch four blocks and set them together in classic nine-patch style with a leafy cotton print. The result is a 12-inch pillow top (which could be enlarged with sashing strips).

🍂 Everything's better with a checkerboard on it. Use this basic three-stitch by three-row border and expand it, alternating the colors as you repeat the three rows. Make it match your home decor, and stitch these checkerboard borders on kitchen or table linens as well as wearables.

🍂 The boy in the tree would make a child's treasured pillow. End the pattern with the checkerboard border and match the color of the border to a checked cotton fabric for the pillow back.

🍂 Play Mother Nature with your own leaves. These classic oak leaves are just asking for colors ranging from green and yellow to burgundy. Sprinkle them on linens or let them fall down the length of a bookmark.

🍂 Stitch an acorn on a jar lid insert and make a treat for your best "nutty" friend.

INSTRUCTIONS

Tape or zigzag edges of Aida cloth to prevent fraying. Find center of Aida cloth and center of chart. Begin stitching there.

Work cross-stitches using three plies of floss. Use two plies of floss to work the featherstitches and the backstitches.

Trim finished stitchery to 6¼×8¼ inches with design centered. Tack fleece to back of stitchery. Center fleece-backed stitchery on board for insert provided with the box. Glue the edges to the back of the board. Mount in box following manufacturer's directions.

NATURALLY YOURS

Lnspire others by stitching a tribute to nature. This design will lift your heart and put the spirit of springtime into even the grayest winter day.

The framed piece includes the text: THE GOAL of LIFE IS LIVING IN AGREEMENT WITH NATURE. ZENO 335-265 BC

THE GOAL OF LIFE
IS LIVING IN AGREEMENT
WITH NATURE.
ZENO 335-263BC

uffle-framed sentiments,
opposite, *speak softly and sweetly from our decorative pillow.*

*Frame this gathering of birds and thoughts, above, as a gift or
accessory. Its message becomes stronger and more personal
when each letter is created with your needle and floss.*

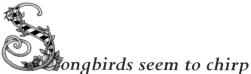 *ongbirds seem to chirp
their happy song as they fly on this linen bellpull, above left.
A cheerful bird feeder makes a great motif to top off a box you fill with
nature's treasures, above right.*

*A cross-stitch band of baskets decorates the harvest-filled container, opposite.
Pack it for a picnic, give it as a gift, or put it on display in your home.*

NATURALLY YOURS PILLOW

ANCHOR		DMC	ANCHOR		DMC	ANCHOR		DMC
002	•	000 White	886		677 Pale old gold	388		842 Beige brown
352	▲	300 Mahogany	901	✳	680 Dark old gold	1044		895 Hunter green
403	■	310 Black	238	⊙	703 Chartreuse	340		920 Copper
9046	◎	321 Christmas red	305	▽	725 Topaz	332	⊕	946 Burnt orange
038	+	335 Rose	158	╱	747 Sky blue	167	◇	3766 Peacock blue
898	#	611 Drab brown	259	−	772 Loden	059	♥	3804 Cyclamen
891	□	676 Light old gold	162	●	825 Bright blue	779	✳	3809 Turquoise

ANCHOR		DMC	
BACKSTITCH			
352	/	300	Mahogany–trees
9046	/	321	Christmas red–hat, cuffs
898	/	611	Drab brown–feedsack, trees, pants
901	/	680	Dark old gold–hair
388	/	842	Beige brown–trees

ANCHOR		DMC	
BACKSTITCH			
1044	/	895	Hunter green–hat
340	/	920	Copper–pants
332	/	946	Burnt orange–birds' feet, pants
403	/	310	Black–all remaining stitches

ANCHOR		DMC	
FRENCH KNOT			
002	○	000	White–berries
352	●	300	Mahogany–squirrels' eyes
403	●	310	Black–birds' eyes

Stitch count: 180 high x 180 wide
Finished design sizes:
28-count fabric – 12⅞ x 12⅞ inches
22-count fabric – 16⅜ x 16⅜ inches
36-count fabric – 10 x 10 inches

NATURALLY YOURS PILLOW

NATURALLY YOURS PILLOW

Look after the comfort of all creatures great and small with this pretty pillow (shown on page 128). Finished pillow is 13½ inches square, not including ruffle.

MATERIALS
FABRICS
18×18-inch piece of 28-count ecru Jubilee cloth
14½×14½-inch piece of fleece for underlining
1½ yards of fabric of choice for ruffle and pillow back
THREADS
Cotton embroidery floss in colors listed in key on pages 132–133
Two additional skeins of DMC 3766
One additional skein of DMC 310, 321, and white

SUPPLIES
Needle; embroidery hoop
1¾ yards of ½-inch-diameter decorative cord with stitching lip
14-inch square pillow form or polyester fiberfill

INSTRUCTIONS
Tape or zigzag edges of Jubilee cloth to prevent fraying. Find the center of the chart and the center of the fabric. Begin stitching there.

Work cross-stitches using three plies of floss over two threads of the Jubilee cloth. Use two plies of floss to work the backstitches and French knots.

Press finished stitchery on wrong side with a warm iron. Trim fabric 1 inch beyond outer border.

Place the 14½-inch square of fleece on the back of cross-stitched piece, basting along outside edge.

Sew cord around stitched pillow front, using ½-inch seam allowance and a zipper foot to stitch close to cord. Begin stitching at center of bottom edge of pillow front, overlapping cord where it meets.

Cut a 14½-inch square from fabric of choice for pillow back. For ruffle, cut 6-inch ruffle strips, piecing as needed to make a total length of 109 inches.

Sew the short ends of the ruffle strips together to form a circle. Fold the ruffle piece in half lengthwise, wrong sides together, and press fold line. Sew a gathering thread through both layers of ruffle ½ inch from raw edges. Pull threads to fit perimeter of pillow front with raw edges even; adjust gathers evenly. Sew ruffle to cross-stitched pillow front, using ½-inch seam allowance.

Sew the pillow front to the back, right sides facing, keeping ruffle tucked inside. Leave an opening for turning. Clip corners, turn right side out, and press.

Insert pillow form or stuff firmly. Whipstitch the opening closed.

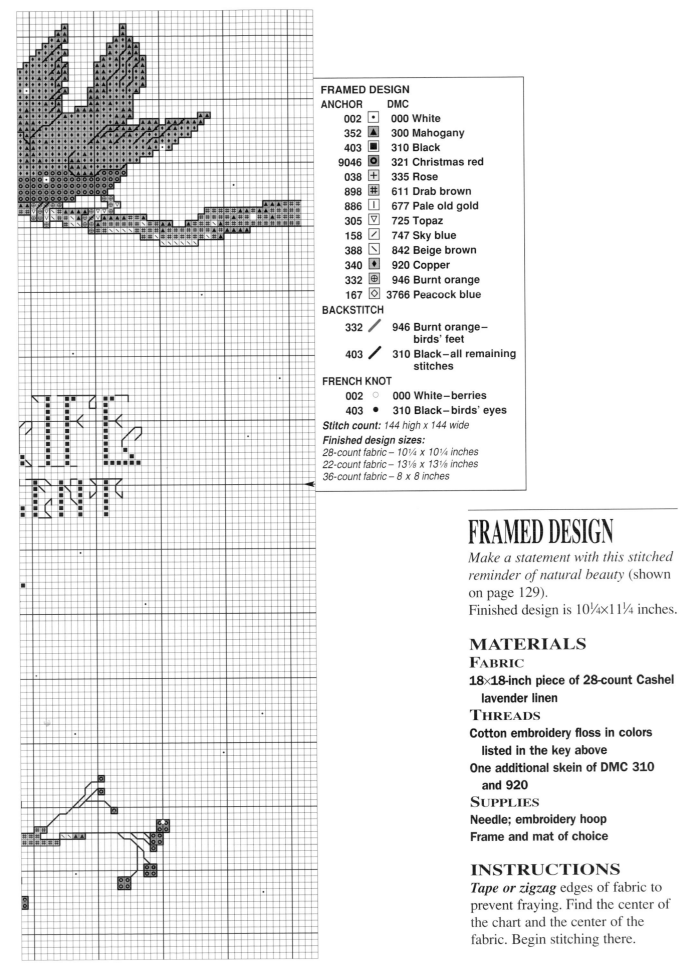

FRAMED DESIGN

ANCHOR		DMC	
002	·	000	White
352	▲	300	Mahogany
403	■	310	Black
9046	◉	321	Christmas red
038	+	335	Rose
898	⊞	611	Drab brown
886	I	677	Pale old gold
305	▽	725	Topaz
158	/	747	Sky blue
388	╲	842	Beige brown
340	◆	920	Copper
332	⊕	946	Burnt orange
167	◇	3766	Peacock blue

BACKSTITCH

332	/	946	Burnt orange–birds' feet
403	/	310	Black–all remaining stitches

FRENCH KNOT

002	○	000	White–berries
403	●	310	Black–birds' eyes

Stitch count: 144 high x 144 wide

Finished design sizes:
28-count fabric – 10¼ x 10¼ inches
22-count fabric – 13⅛ x 13⅛ inches
36-count fabric – 8 x 8 inches

FRAMED DESIGN

Make a statement with this stitched reminder of natural beauty (shown on page 129).
Finished design is 10¼×11¼ inches.

MATERIALS

FABRIC
18×18-inch piece of 28-count Cashel lavender linen

THREADS
Cotton embroidery floss in colors listed in the key above
One additional skein of DMC 310 and 920

SUPPLIES
Needle; embroidery hoop
Frame and mat of choice

INSTRUCTIONS

Tape or zigzag edges of fabric to prevent fraying. Find the center of the chart and the center of the fabric. Begin stitching there.

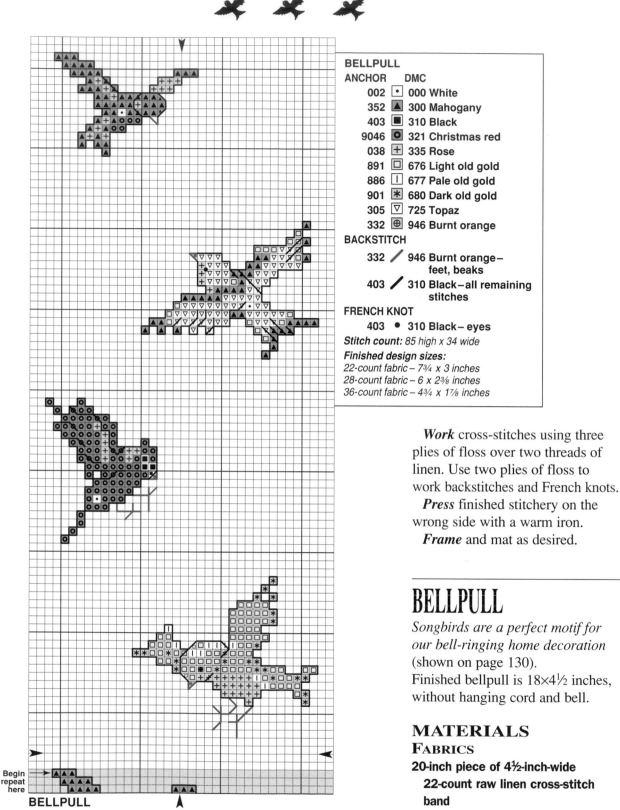

BELLPULL

ANCHOR		DMC	
002	·	000	White
352	▲	300	Mahogany
403	■	310	Black
9046	⊙	321	Christmas red
038	+	335	Rose
891	□	676	Light old gold
886			677	Pale old gold
901	✳	680	Dark old gold
305	▽	725	Topaz
332	⊕	946	Burnt orange

BACKSTITCH

332	/	946	Burnt orange– feet, beaks
403	/	310	Black–all remaining stitches

FRENCH KNOT

403	•	310	Black– eyes

Stitch count: 85 high x 34 wide

Finished design sizes:
22-count fabric – 7¾ x 3 inches
28-count fabric – 6 x 2⅜ inches
36-count fabric – 4¾ x 1⅞ inches

Begin repeat here

BELLPULL

Work cross-stitches using three plies of floss over two threads of linen. Use two plies of floss to work backstitches and French knots.

Press finished stitchery on the wrong side with a warm iron.

Frame and mat as desired.

BELLPULL

Songbirds are a perfect motif for our bell-ringing home decoration (shown on page 130). Finished bellpull is 18×4½ inches, without hanging cord and bell.

MATERIALS

FABRICS

20-inch piece of 4½-inch-wide 22-count raw linen cross-stitch band

20×5-inch piece of felted imitation suede fabric

THREADS

Cotton embroidery floss in colors listed in the key above

SUPPLIES
Needle
Bellpull hanger of choice
Bell of choice
⅔ yard of ¼-inch-diameter cord
Two 3-inch matching tassels
Tacky glue

INSTRUCTIONS

Tape or zigzag ends of cross-stitch band. Find the center of the cross-stitch band and the center of the chart. Begin stitching there.

Work cross-stitches using three plies of floss over two threads of the linen cross-stitch band. Use two plies of floss to work the backstitches and French knots.

Repeat chart once to stitch other half of bellpull.

Fold the fabric in half lengthwise with right sides together. Stitch across the bottom end, making a ¼-inch seam. Turn to right side and press to form the pointed end.

Cut suede backing ⅛ inch larger than completed cross-stitched linen. Glue linen to suede, using a small amount of glue on edges only.

Turn 1½ inches at top of the cross-stitch band and suede backing to the back with wrong sides together. Stitch a casing to accommodate the bellpull holder.

Insert the bellpull holder. Tie cording to each end of the holder, then loop cording around holder. At the center of the cording, tie a knot to form a hanging loop. Tie a tassel on each end of the holder. Tack a bell to the center of the point at the bottom of the bellpull.

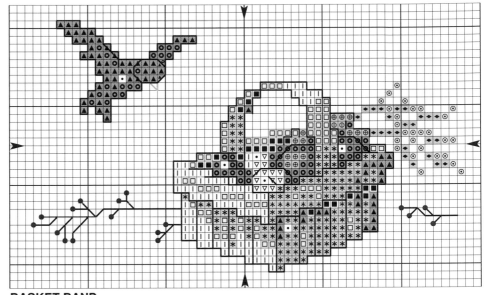

BASKET BAND

BASKET BAND

Decorate a country basket with a band of stitched baskets (shown on page 131).
Finished band is 3×44 inches.

MATERIALS
FABRIC
1⅓ yards (or desired length) 3-inch-wide 14-count red-edged cross-stitch band
THREADS
Cotton embroidery floss in colors listed in the key at right
SUPPLIES
Needle; basket of choice
Fabric liner of choice

INSTRUCTIONS
Measure half of the basket circumference from handle to handle. Add at least 2 inches to the measurement and cut 2 pieces of cross-stitch band to that length.

Find center of one of the pieces of cross-stitch band and the center of the chart. Begin stitching there.

Work cross-stitches using three plies of floss. Use two plies to work

BASKET BAND		
ANCHOR	DMC	
002	⊡	000 White
352	▲	300 Mahogany
403	■	310 Black
9046	⊙	321 Christmas red
891	▢	676 Light old gold
886	❘	677 Pale old gold
901	✱	680 Dark old gold
238	⊚	703 Chartreuse
305	▽	725 Topaz
332	⊕	946 Burnt orange
BACKSTITCH		
886	╱	677 Pale old gold – bird's beak
403	╱	310 Black – all remaining stitches
FRENCH KNOT		
9046	●	321 Christmas red – berries

Stitch count: 32 high x 55 wide
Finished design sizes:
14-count fabric – 2¼ x 3⅞ inches
11-count fabric – 2⅞ x 5 inches
18-count fabric – 1¾ x 3⅛ inches

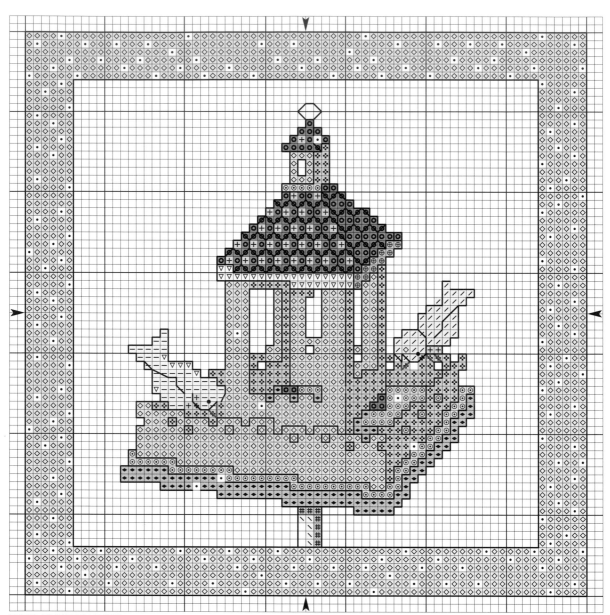

BIRD FEEDER BOX

the backstitches and French knots. Repeat stitching the chart as needed to reach desired length.

Repeat with second band.

Line basket as desired, making a 4-inch skirt to hang over the top edge of the basket.

Tack cross-stitch band to skirt of the basket lining. Turn under raw edges at ends of band and whipstitch in place where lining skirt is split for basket handle.

BIRD FEEDER BOX

ANCHOR		DMC	
002	·	000	White
9046	◉	321	Christmas red
038	+	335	Rose
898	✚	611	Drab brown
238	◉	703	Chartreuse
305	▽	725	Topaz
158	⁄	747	Sky blue
259	—	772	Loden
388	◿	842	Beige brown
1044	◆	895	Hunter green
332	⊕	946	Burnt orange
167	◇	3766	Peacock blue
779	❖	3809	Turquoise

ANCHOR		DMC	
BACKSTITCH			
332	╱	946	Burnt orange– birds' feet, beaks
403	╱	310	Black–all remaining stitches
FRENCH KNOT			
403	●	310	Black–birds' eyes

Stitch count: 70 high x 70 wide
Finished design sizes:
14-count fabric – 5 x 5 inches
11-count fabric – 6⅜ x 6⅜ inches
18-count fabric – 3⅞ x 3⅞ inches

BIRD FEEDER BOX

Adorn your treasure box with a happy gathering place for birds (shown on page 130). Finished design is 5×5 inches.

MATERIALS

FABRICS
9×9-inch piece of 14-count Floba cloth
Two 6×6-inch pieces of fleece

THREADS
Cotton embroidery floss in colors listed in the key on page 140

SUPPLIES
Needle; embroidery hoop
Faux box with 5-inch-square opening
⅔ yard of ⅛-inch-diameter black cord
Tacky glue

INSTRUCTIONS

Tape or zigzag edges of Floba cloth. Find the center of the chart and the center of the Floba cloth. Begin stitching there.

Work cross-stitches using three plies of floss. Use two plies to work backstitches and French knots.

Press stitchery on the wrong side with a warm iron.

Trim 1½ inches from each side of Floba cloth, making a 6-inch square with design centered. Place a 6×6-inch piece of fleece on wrong side of the Floba cloth. Use other piece of fleece to cover board supplied with box. Turn ½ inch fleece to back of board and glue in place.

Center fleece-backed Floba cloth on top of fleece-covered board. Glue outer edges to back of board, folding and trimming corners for neat appearance. Follow the manufacturer's directions to fit the stitchery into the box.

Add cord around outside edge with a bit of glue. Push cord down into channel; butt ends together.

Breit Ideas

Naturally, you'll find many stitching opportunities with this cheerful songbird design.

Dinner-is-served place mats will brighten your family table–especially in the wintertime. Use the Bird Feeder Box chart to stitch one corner of your place mat and add a few songbirds on other corners or napkins.

Baby's bib is another good place for a bird feeder motif. The happy ritual of feeding a child definitely is living in agreement with nature.

Feather your bed with cross-stitched songbird quilt blocks. Set finished 4-inch cross-stitch blocks with blocks of colorful cotton prints.

Dress a window with songbirds. (The window with the view of the bird feeder where the cat sits all day would be the best one.) Use a cross-stitch band to stitch bright-colored birds on curtain tiebacks or to edge a valance.

A basketful of best wishes can be sent with gifts adorned with cross-stitch baskets. Use the Basket Band chart to stitch kitchen towels, pot holders, and other prefinished items.

Stitch a table runner with the birds on the branches from the Framed Design chart. Use the top branch on one end and the bottom branch on the other, leaving as much space as desired in the center.

CROSS COUNTRY

Celebrate winter as well as the holidays with this Mary Engelbreit greeting. High-energy fun is combined with a quiet, snow-covered setting and a thoughtful message to create many gift-stitching opportunities.

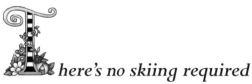

*here's no skiing required
in order to enjoy the trip to a friend's house. In fact, you don't even need snow.
Even Sunbelt residents will prize this framed message, opposite,
of energy and determination.*

*Snow falls gently on tall trees and a cozy home, making a perfect scene for the
base of a paperweight, above. Holly and berries always add a festive touch
to greetings, so use these motifs for personalized cards, above, or stitch
them for your holiday decorating.*

*C*hildren often love the wrapping
on a present as much as the gift—now the grown-up kids can join the fun.
This silver-sparkled fabric featuring your stitchery of a skier with a backpack
of gifts, **opposite**, hides a hard-to-wrap present with style.

Deliver your deep sentiments to a faraway friend with this especially
thoughtful gift, **above**. The handcarved double mat accents
your stitches and your message.

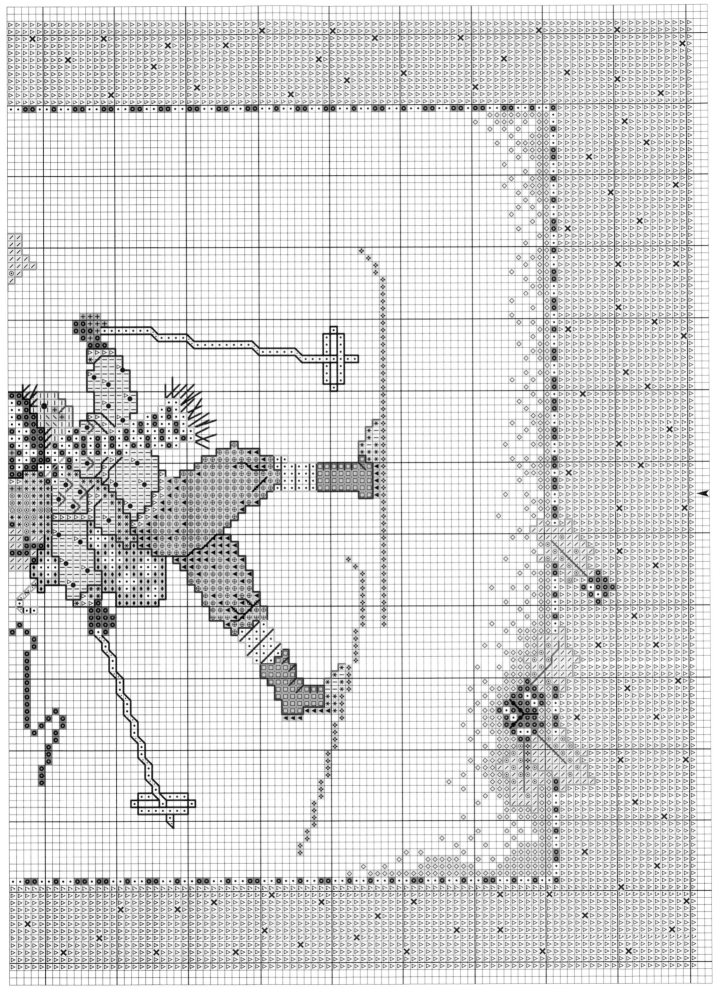

CROSS COUNTRY SAMPLER

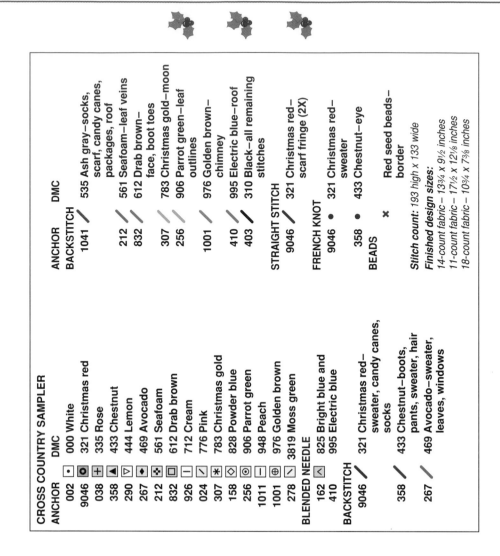

CROSS COUNTRY SAMPLER

ANCHOR							DMC	
002	•						000	White
9046	◉						321	Christmas red
038	+						335	Rose
358	◀						433	Chestnut
290	▷						444	Lemon
267	◆						469	Avocado
212	✛						561	Seafoam
832	□						612	Drab brown
926	—						712	Cream
024	◹						776	Pink
307	✳						783	Christmas gold
158	◇						828	Powder blue
256	◉						906	Parrot green
1011	Ｉ						948	Peach
1001	⊕						976	Golden brown
278	◿						3819	Moss green

BLENDED NEEDLE

162	◁	825	Bright blue and
410		995	Electric blue

BACKSTITCH

9046	╱	321	Christmas red–sweater, candy canes, socks
358	╱	433	Chestnut–boots, pants, sweater, hair
267	╱	469	Avocado–sweater, leaves, windows

ANCHOR		DMC	
BACKSTITCH			
1041	╱	535	Ash gray–socks, scarf, candy canes, packages, roof
212	╱	561	Seafoam–leaf veins
832	╱	612	Drab brown–face, boot toes
307	╱	783	Christmas gold–moon
256	╱	906	Parrot green–leaf outlines
1001	╱	976	Golden brown–chimney
410	╱	995	Electric blue–roof
403	╱	310	Black–all remaining stitches
STRAIGHT STITCH			
9046	╱	321	Christmas red–scarf fringe (2X)
FRENCH KNOT			
9046	•	321	Christmas red–sweater
358	•	433	Chestnut–eye
BEADS			
	✕		Red seed beads–border

Stitch count: 193 high x 133 wide
Finished design sizes:
14-count fabric – 13¾ x 9½ inches
11-count fabric – 17½ x 12⅛ inches
18-count fabric – 10¾ x 7⅞ inches

CROSS COUNTRY SAMPLER

It's the thought that counts and ensures that this stitchery will be enjoyed year-round (shown on page 144).
Finished design is 13¾×9½ inches.

MATERIALS
FABRIC
20×16-inch piece of 14-count white Aida cloth

THREADS
Cotton embroidery floss in colors listed in the key above
Five additional skeins of DMC 444
Two additional skeins of DMC 712
One additional skein of DMC 321 and 828

SUPPLIES
Needle; embroidery hoop
Red seed beads (approximately 175)
½-inch-diameter silver and white pom-pom
Mat and frame of choice

INSTRUCTIONS
Tape or zigzag edges of white Aida cloth to prevent fraying. Find the center of the chart and center of Aida cloth. Begin stitching there.

Work cross-stitches using three plies of floss. Use two plies of DMC 825 and one ply of DMC 995 to work blended needle stitches. Use two plies of floss to work the straight stitches, backstitches, and French knots.

Add seed beads as indicated on chart. Sew pom-pom to top of hat. Mat and frame as desired.

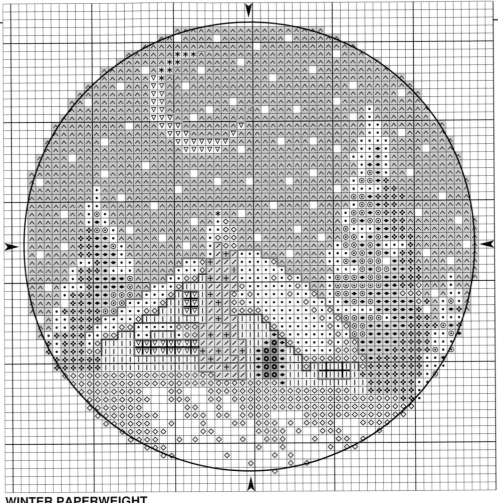

WINTER PAPERWEIGHT

WINTER PAPERWEIGHT

Snowflakes on a dark sky are perfect for this easy-finish showcase for your stitchery (shown on page 145).

The finished paperweight has a 3¼-inch-diameter base.

MATERIALS

FABRIC
6×6-inch piece of 18-count white Aida cloth

THREADS
Cotton embroidery floss in colors listed in the key at left

SUPPLIES
Needle; embroidery hoop
Glass paperweight with 3¼-inch-diameter base
Needlework finisher
Crafts glue

INSTRUCTIONS

Tape or zigzag edges of white Aida cloth to prevent fraying. Find the center of the chart and the center of the Aida cloth. Begin stitching there.

Work cross-stitches using two plies of floss. Work blended needle using one ply of each floss color. Use two plies of floss to work the backstitches for the windows. Use one ply of floss to work remaining backstitches.

Trim completed stitchery, using the circle on chart as a guide. Using needlework finisher, secure the threads at the edge of stitchery. Follow manufacturer's directions to glue stitchery to paperweight base and complete.

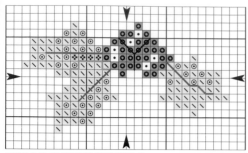

HOLLY CARDS MOTIF A

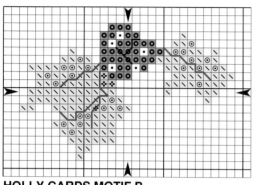

HOLLY CARDS MOTIF B

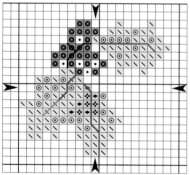

HOLLY CARDS MOTIF C

HOLLY CARDS			
ANCHOR		**DMC**	
002	·	000	White
9046	◉	321	Christmas red
267	◆	469	Avocado
212	✛	561	Seafoam
256	◎	906	Parrot green
278	⟍	3819	Moss green
BACKSTITCH			
403	╱	310	Black–berry
267	╱	469	Avocado–leaf veins
212	╱	561	Seafoam–leaf veins
256	╱	906	Parrot green–leaf veins

HOLLY CARDS

These holly-berry motifs have countless uses throughout the holidays (shown on page 145). Finished motifs are approximately 1½×2 inches.

MATERIALS

For one card

FABRICS

3×4-inch piece of 14-count Aida Plus

2×3-inch piece of green felt

THREADS

Cotton embroidery floss in colors listed in the key below left

SUPPLIES

Needle; crafts glue

12-inch piece of ⅛-inch-wide red satin ribbon

Card of choice

INSTRUCTIONS

Find the center of one of the holly charts and the center of the Aida Plus. Begin stitching there.

Work cross-stitches using three plies of floss. Use two plies of floss to work the backstitches.

Trim around the Aida Plus, one square from stitching.

Use two plies of floss to overcast around all raw edges.

Glue completed motif to the center of the piece of green felt. Trim felt, leaving approximately ⅛ inch around the stitched motif.

Tie red ribbon into a bow and tack to the top of the motif; glue motif to the card. Or, use ribbon to tie the motif to the card through a hole punched in the card.

FRIEND'S MESSAGE

The stitching, as well as the journey, goes quickly when you deliver this message to a friend (shown on page 147). Finished design is 6⅜×4¼ inches.

MATERIALS

FABRIC

12×10-inch piece of 28-count ecru Quaker cloth

THREADS

Cotton embroidery floss in colors listed in the key on page 153

SUPPLIES

Needle; embroidery hoop

Frame and mat of choice

INSTRUCTIONS

Tape or zigzag edges of Quaker cloth to prevent fraying. Find the center of the chart and center of the Quaker cloth. Begin stitching there.

Work cross-stitches using three plies of floss over two threads of the Quaker cloth. Use two plies of floss to work the backstitches.

Press completed stitching on the wrong side with a warm iron. Mat and frame as desired.

Motif A stitch count: 14 high x 26 wide

Motif A finished design sizes:
14-count fabric – 1 x 1⅞ inches
11-count fabric – 1¼ x 2⅜ inches
18-count fabric – ¾ x 1⅜ inches

Motif B stitch count: 17 high x 27 wide

Motif B finished design sizes:
14-count fabric – 1¼ x 1⅞ inches
11-count fabric – 1⅝ x 2⅜ inches
18-count fabric – ⅞ x 1½ inches

Motif C stitch count: 17 high x 19 wide

Motif C finished design sizes:
14-count fabric – 1¼ x 1⅜ inches
11-count fabric – 1⅝ x 1¾ inches
18-count fabric – ⅞ x 1⅛ inches

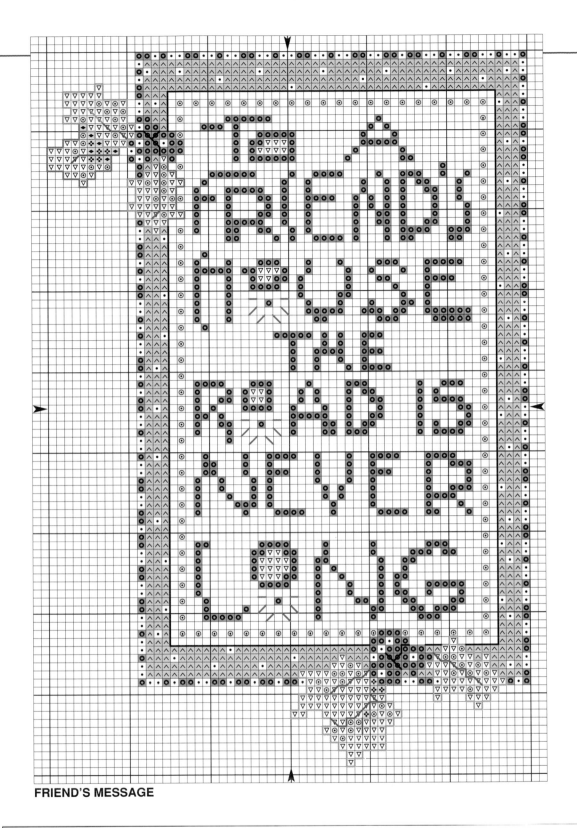

FRIEND'S MESSAGE

FRIEND'S MESSAGE

ANCHOR		DMC	
002	·	000	White
9046	◎	321	Christmas red
290	▽	444	Lemon
267	◆	469	Avocado
212	✤	561	Seafoam
256	⊙	906	Parrot green
410	∧	995	Electric blue

ANCHOR		DMC	
BACKSTITCH			
403	╱	310	Black—berries, border
267	╱	469	Avocado—saying, leaf outlines, veins
212	╱	561	Seafoam—leaf veins
256	╱	906	Parrot green— leaf outlines, veins

Stitch count: 89 high x 60 wide
Finished design sizes:
28-count fabric—6⅜ x 4¼ inches
22-count fabric—8⅛ x 5½ inches
36-count fabric—5 x 3⅜ inches

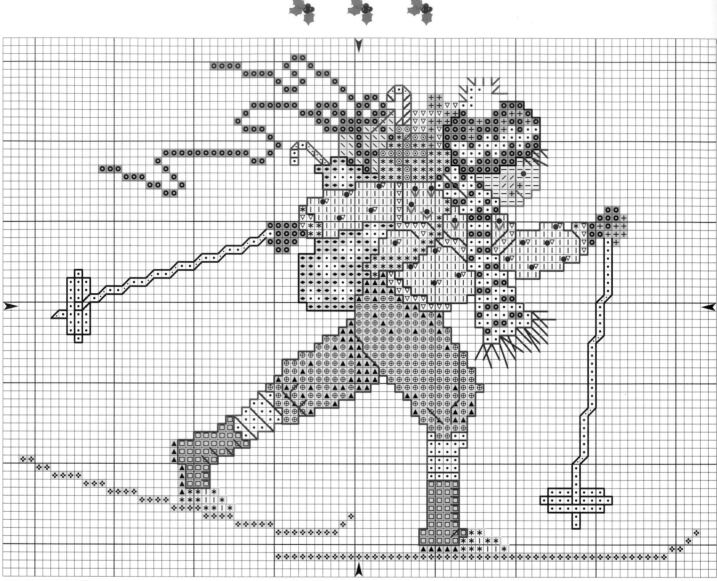

SKIER GIFT BAG

SKIER GIFT BAG

ANCHOR		DMC
002	·	000 White
9046	⊙	321 Christmas red
038	+	335 Rose
358	▲	433 Chestnut
290	▽	444 Lemon
267	◆	469 Avocado
212	✤	561 Seafoam
832	▫	612 Drab brown
926			712 Cream
024	/	776 Pink
307	*	783 Christmas gold
256	⊚	906 Parrot green
1011	−	948 Peach
1001	⊕	976 Golden brown
278	◺	3819 Moss green

ANCHOR		DMC
BACKSTITCH		
403	/	310 Black – hat, bag, ski poles
9046	/	321 Christmas red – sweater, candy canes, socks
358	/	433 Chestnut – boots, pants, sweater, hair
267	/	469 Avocado – sweater
1041	/	535 Ash gray – socks, scarf, candy canes, packages
832	/	612 Drab brown – face
307	/	783 Christmas gold – boot toes

ANCHOR		DMC
STRAIGHT STITCH		
9046	/	321 Christmas red – scarf fringe (2X)
FRENCH KNOT		
358	●	433 Chestnut – eye
BEADS		
	●	Red seed beads – sweater

Stitch count: 63 high x 85 wide
Finished design sizes:
20-count fabric –6⅜ x 8½ inches
28-count fabric – 4½ x 6⅛ inches
36-count fabric – 3½ x 4¾ inches

SKIER GIFT BAG

Silver threads woven into the fabric make this gift bag even more dazzling (shown on page 146). Finished bag is 14×8×3 inches.

MATERIALS
FABRICS
17×25-inch piece of 20-count silver/white Valerie cloth

17×25-inch piece of fabric of choice for lining

THREADS
Cotton embroidery floss in colors listed in the key on page 154

SUPPLIES
Needle; embroidery hoop

Red glass seed beads (approximately 25)

½-inch-diameter red pom-pom

INSTRUCTIONS

Tape or zigzag edges of Valerie cloth to prevent fraying. Find the center of the Valerie cloth; mark a spot approximately 1 inch lower. (The starting spot on the fabric will be approximately 9 inches from the top and 8 inches from the bottom.) Find the center of the chart and begin stitching at the spot marked.

Work cross-stitches using three plies of floss over two threads of the Valerie cloth. Use two plies of floss to work the backstitches, straight stitches, and French knots.

Add glass seed beads. Sew red pom-pom to the top of the hat.

Stitch lining fabric to top of the cross-stitched fabric (along 25-inch length) with right sides together.

Stitch center back seam of bag and lining, leaving an opening in the lining seam for turning.

Stitch bag bottom seam. With bottom seam centered, fold bag to box bottom corners. Stitch across the end, making a 3½-inch seam perpendicular to the bottom seam. Trim away excess fabric. Repeat for other end of the bag bottom. Repeat for the lining.

Turn the bag right side out. Whipstitch the opening in the lining closed.

Breit Ideas

Use the energy inspired by this design to keep moving on stitching projects for holiday gifts.

❧ Quick-to-stitch holly and berry motifs will add your personal stamp to gift tags or place cards for the table. Stitch a few holly leaves on a cross-stitch band to make keepsake bows for gifts.

❧ Use the Friend's Message chart to stitch the front of a map case (you can omit the holly leaves if desired). Use a folded road map to determine the size of the case, and refer to instructions for the eyeglasses case on page 166 for construction help.

❧ Stitch the house, trees, moon, and snow-sprinkled sky for a small framed picture. Send this serene scene to a friend in the South.

❧ Not quite a checkerboard, the dot-and-dash one-row border on this sampler produces a nice effect. This finishing technique may be just what you need for some of your table linens.

❧ Try some special touches for added dimension. Stitching from the Skier Gift Bag chart, use sticks for the skis, wires for the poles, and real ribbon for the bows coming out of the backpack in addition to the pom-pom on the hat and beads on the sweater.

Jolly
Holiday

anta's dream coat sets the
tone for a Christmas full of happy surprises. Cherries and
checkerboards, bunnies and flowers evoke a fresh holiday attitude
and provide many stitching opportunities.

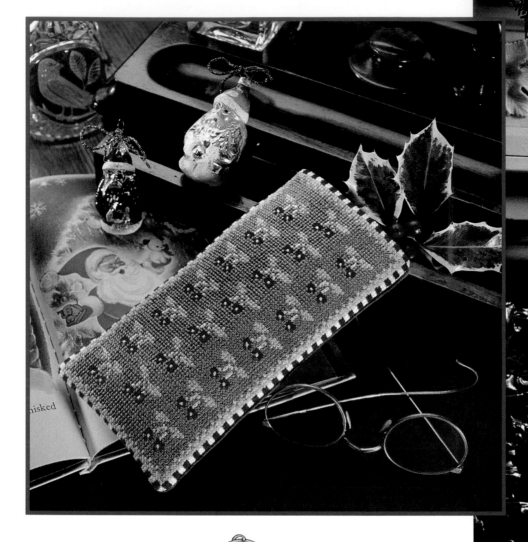

Cherries are a Mary
Engelbreit signature design and make a delightful
pattern—on Santa's coat or any home stitchery. For a
classic, personal gift, stitch cherries on an
easy-to-make eyeglasses case, above.

The delight of Christmas is captured in this banner,
opposite. Easy to assemble, it's a great option
to framing a sampler for seasonal home decor.
In your entrance hall or above your fireplace, Santa
waves a happy greeting.

Rabbits *sport sweaters and Santa hats in Christmas enthusiasm. We named these bunnies, above, Hoppy, Happy, and Harey and believe they'll jazz up your holiday stitching.*

Stitch just the cuff of an elegant Christmas stocking, **opposite,** *to deck your mantel. Our kind and friendly Santa seems to be promising to old and young alike, "I'm on my way!"*

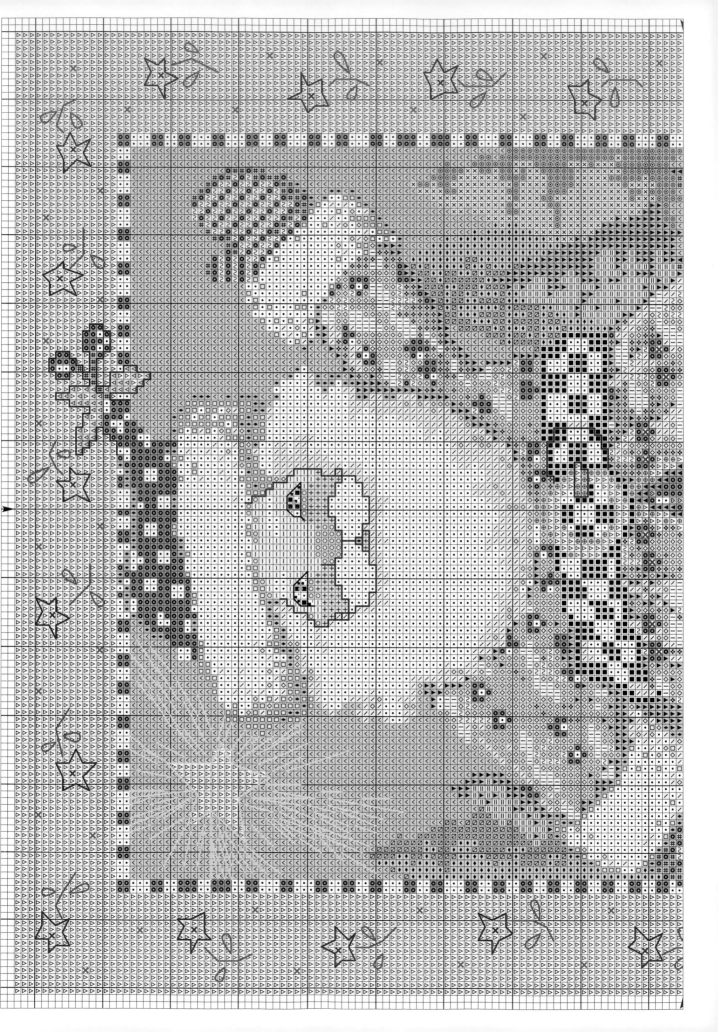

JOLLY HOLIDAY BANNER

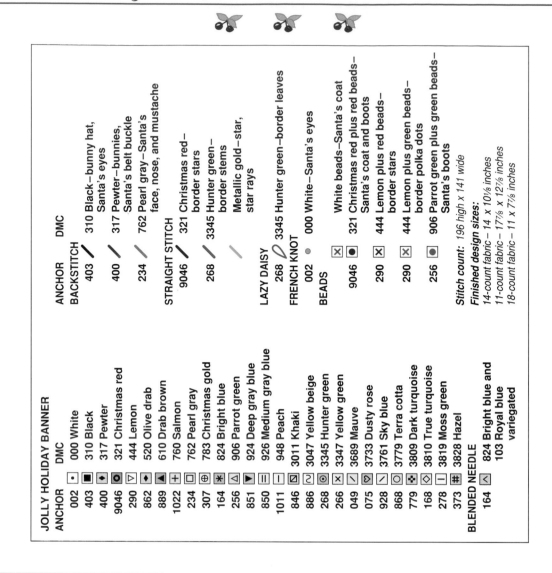

JOLLY HOLIDAY BANNER

ANCHOR	DMC		
002	·	000	White
403	■	310	Black
400	◆	317	Pewter
9046	◉	321	Christmas red
290	▷	444	Lemon
862	◆	520	Olive drab
889	◀	610	Drab brown
1022	+	760	Salmon
234	□	762	Pearl gray
307	⊕	783	Christmas gold
164	✳	824	Bright blue
256	◁	906	Parrot green
851	▶	924	Deep gray blue
850	‖	926	Medium gray blue
1011			948	Peach
846	▨	3011	Khaki
886	⟨	3047	Yellow beige
268	◉	3345	Hunter green
266	✕	3347	Yellow green
049	╱	3689	Mauve
075	▷	3733	Dusty rose
928	╱	3761	Sky blue
868	○	3779	Terra cotta
779	✦	3809	Dark turquoise
168	◇	3810	True turquoise
278	—	3819	Moss green
373	⊞	3828	Hazel

BLENDED NEEDLE

164	◁	824	Bright blue and
103			Royal blue variegated

BACKSTITCH

403	╱	310	Black–bunny hat, Santa's eyes
400	╱	317	Pewter–bunnies, Santa's belt buckle
234	╱	762	Pearl gray–Santa's face, nose, and mustache

STRAIGHT STITCH

9046	╱	321	Christmas red–border stars
268	╱	3345	Hunter green–border stems
			Metallic gold–star, star rays

LAZY DAISY

268	⟋	3345	Hunter green–border leaves

FRENCH KNOT

002	●	000	White–Santa's eyes

BEADS

	⊠		White beads–Santa's coat
9046	●	321	Christmas red plus red beads–Santa's coat and boots
290	⊠	444	Lemon plus red beads–border stars
290	⊠	444	Lemon plus green beads–border polka dots
256	●	906	Parrot green plus green beads–Santa's boots

Stitch count: 196 high x 141 wide
Finished design sizes:
14-count fabric – 14 x 10⅛ inches
11-count fabric – 17⅞ x 12⅞ inches
18-count fabric – 11 x 7⅞ inches

JOLLY HOLIDAY BANNER

Greet everyone who comes to your home with this happy, waving Santa (shown on page 159). Finished banner is 25×16 inches, not including tassel.

MATERIALS

FABRICS
20×16-inch piece of 14-count white Aida cloth
1 yard of green velveteen
1 yard of cotton fabric for backing

THREADS
Cotton embroidery floss in colors listed in the key above

Four additional skeins of DMC 444
Two additional skeins of DMC 321 and white
One additional skein of DMC 103 310, 824, and 3810

SUPPLIES
Needle; embroidery hoop
Seed beads (approximately 105 red, 100 green, and 35 white)
29×17-inch piece of fleece
2 yards of 1-inch-wide blue grosgrain ribbon
2 yards of ⅜-inch-wide red flat braid
2 yards of ½-inch-wide red and gold flat braid
18-inch piece of ½-inch-diameter dowel
1 yard of ⅜-inch-diameter gold metallic cord
Four 3-inch-long red tassels

INSTRUCTIONS
Tape or zigzag edges of Aida cloth to prevent fraying. Find center of the chart and center of the fabric. Begin stitching there.

Work cross-stitches using three plies of floss. Use one ply each of DMC 103 and DMC 824 to work blended needle stitches. Use one strand of gold metallic thread for straight stitches around star. Use two plies of floss to work the other straight stitches, backstitches, French knots and lazy daisy stitches.

Cut a 29×17-inch piece of green velveteen. Mark center of one 17-inch end and a point on each side, 9 inches from the end.

Mark straight lines from the center point to side points and cut to make the pointed end for banner.

Cut backing fabric piece the same as the velveteen. Trim fleece to same dimensions and baste fleece to back of velveteen.

Trim stitched Aida cloth ½ inch outside the stitching. Center stitchery on velveteen piece, 9 inches above pointed end and 7 inches below top. Sew in place.

Cover edges of Aida cloth with grosgrain ribbon. Stitch both edges of ribbon, mitering the corners.

Stitch red braid on top of ribbon at edge of stitchery.

Place backing fabric on top of banner, right sides together. Stitch around sides and pointed end, leaving top edge open, using ½-inch seam allowance. Clip corners and turn.

Stitch red and gold flat braid around banner, ¼ inch from edges.

Fold 3½ inches at the top of the banner to the back side. Topstitch to form a casing 1¼ inches below the fold line.

Insert dowel in casing. Tie gold cord to each end. Tie tassel on each end of dowel. Tack two tassels to bottom point.

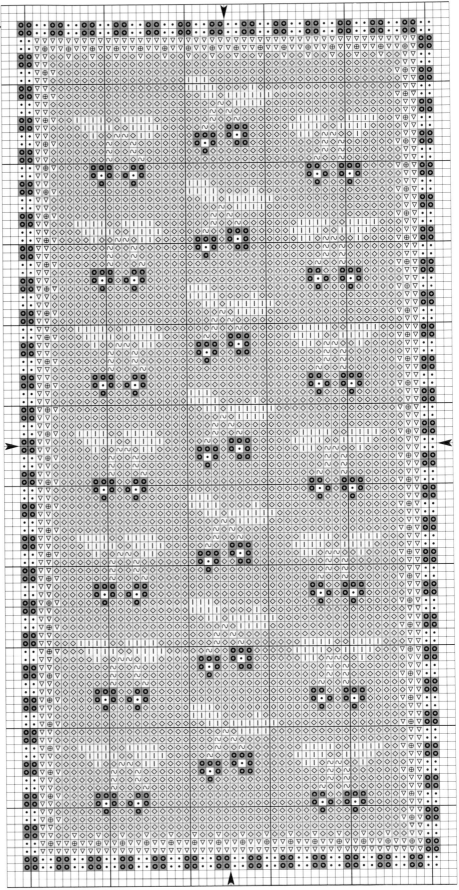

EYEGLASSES CASE

ANCHOR		DMC
002	·	000 White
9046	◉	321 Christmas red
290	▽	444 Lemon
307	⊕	783 Christmas gold
886	∿	3047 Yellow beige
168	◇	3810 True turquoise
278			3819 Moss green

Stitch count: 106 high x 52 wide

Finished design sizes:
14-count fabric – 7½ x 3¾ inches
11-count fabric – 9¾ x 4¾ inches
18-count fabric – 6 x 3 inches

EYEGLASSES CASE

EYEGLASSES CASE

Stitch a cheery, cherry eyeglasses case (shown on page 158) for your best friend's Christmas gift. Finished case is 7½×3¾ inches.

MATERIALS

FABRICS
12×8-inch piece of 14-count white Aida cloth

11×5-inch piece of velveteen

8×9½-inch piece of fabric for lining

THREADS
Cotton embroidery floss in colors listed in the key on page 165

SUPPLIES
Needle; embroidery hoop

INSTRUCTIONS

Tape or zigzag edges of Aida cloth to prevent fraying. Find the center of the chart and the center of the fabric. Begin stitching there.

Work cross-stitches using three plies of floss.

Trim Aida cloth, leaving ½ inch unstitched edge around stitchery.

Cut a 4¾×2-inch piece of velveteen. Sew velveteen strip to top of stitchery with right sides together, using ½-inch seam.

Cut a 9×4¾-inch piece of velveteen for back of case. Cut two 8×4¾-inch pieces of lining fabric.

Sew a lining piece to the top edge (the velveteen strip) of front of case. Sew a lining piece to the top edge of the velveteen piece for the back of the case.

Place case front and lining on top of case back and lining with right sides together. Stitch around all sides, using ½-inch seams and leaving an opening in one side for turning.

Clip corners and turn to right side. Whipstitch the opening closed. Tuck lining inside case. This will leave a 1-inch facing of velveteen inside the top of the case.

CHRISTMAS ORNAMENTS

Trim your tree with bunnies. Long-eared friends of Santa—Hoppy, Happy, and Harey—make unique ornaments (shown on page 160). Finished ornaments are each approximately 4×4 inches.

MATERIALS
(For each ornament)

FABRIC
8×8-inch piece of 25-count Floba cloth

THREADS
Cotton embroidery floss in colors listed in the key for each ornament (at right and on page 168)

SUPPLIES
Needle; embroidery hoop

5×5-inch piece of paper-backed iron-on adhesive

10×5-inch piece of red felt

½ yard of ¼-inch-diameter gold cord

Crafts glue

½ yard of ¼-inch-wide flat braid

Two ½-inch-diameter gold jingle bells

½ yard of ⅜-inch-wide red satin ribbon

INSTRUCTIONS

Tape or zigzag edges of Floba cloth to prevent fraying. Find the center of the desired ornament chart and the center of the fabric. Begin stitching there.

Work cross-stitches using three plies of floss over two threads of the Floba cloth. Use two plies of floss to work the backstitches.

Using the ornament outlines on page 167, trace shape for selected design and transfer to paper-backed adhesive. Cut out shape, center on back of stitchery, and fuse in place. Trim Floba cloth to edge of paper-backed adhesive. Using the trimmed Floba cloth as a pattern, cut two pieces of felt, adding ¼-inch allowance on all sides.

"HAREY" ORNAMENT		
ANCHOR		DMC
002	•	000 White
403	■	310 Black
400	◆	317 Pewter
9046	◉	321 Christmas red
234	□	762 Pearl gray
049	╱	3689 Mauve
075	♡	3733 Dusty rose
928	◳	3761 Sky blue
168	◈	3810 True turquoise
BACKSTITCH		
403	╱	310 Black—all stitches

Stitch count: 25 high x 33 wide
Finished design sizes:
25-count fabric – 2 x 2⅝ inches
22-count fabric – 2¼ x 3 inches
36-count fabric – 1½ x 1⅞ inches

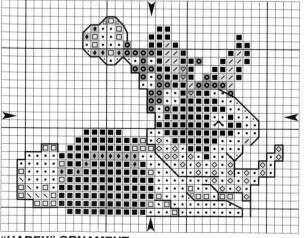

"HAREY" ORNAMENT

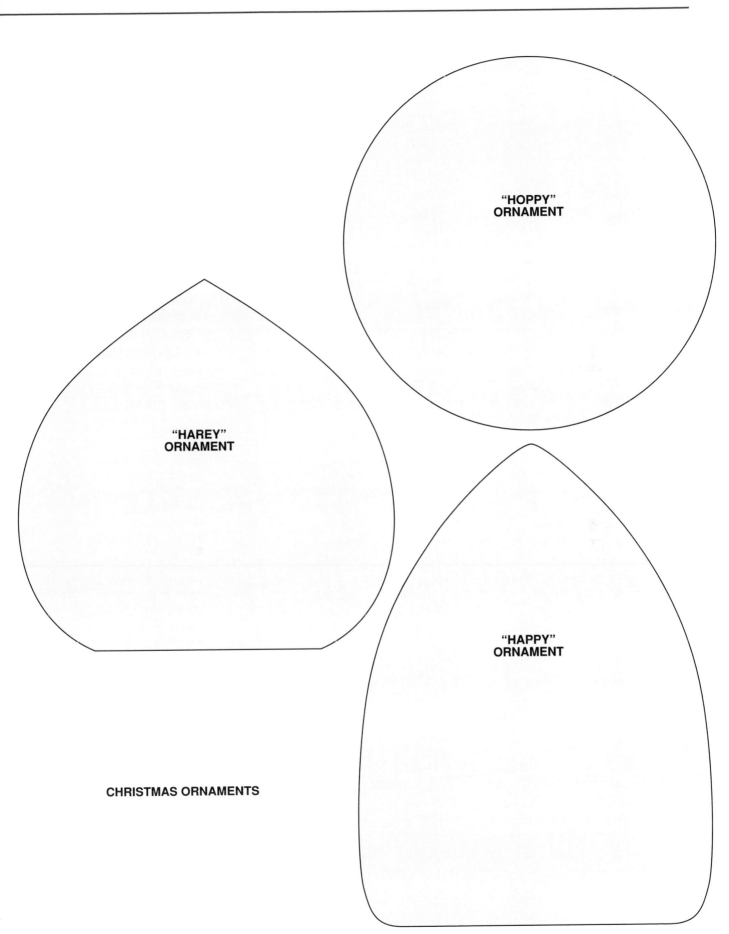

"HOPPY"
ORNAMENT

"HAREY"
ORNAMENT

"HAPPY"
ORNAMENT

CHRISTMAS ORNAMENTS

167

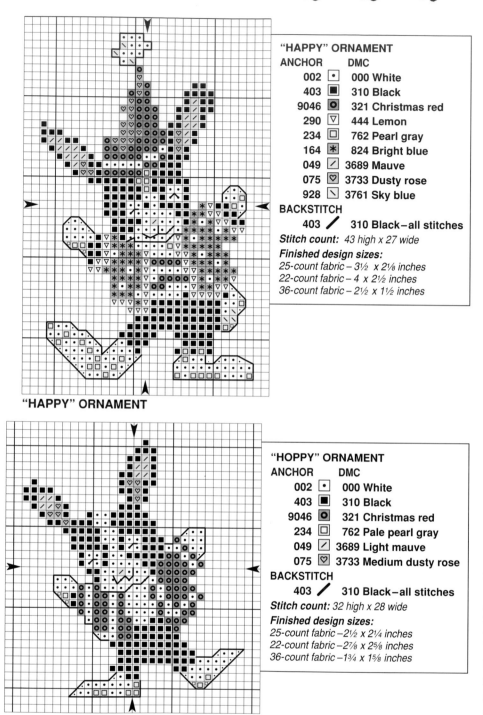

"HAPPY" ORNAMENT

"HAPPY" ORNAMENT		
ANCHOR		DMC
002	·	000 White
403	■	310 Black
9046	◉	321 Christmas red
290	▽	444 Lemon
234	□	762 Pearl gray
164	✳	824 Bright blue
049	╱	3689 Mauve
075	♡	3733 Dusty rose
928	◹	3761 Sky blue

BACKSTITCH

403	╱	310 Black–all stitches

Stitch count: 43 high x 27 wide

Finished design sizes:
25-count fabric – 3½ x 2⅛ inches
22-count fabric – 4 x 2½ inches
36-count fabric – 2½ x 1½ inches

"HOPPY" ORNAMENT

"HOPPY" ORNAMENT		
ANCHOR		DMC
002	·	000 White
403	■	310 Black
9046	◉	321 Christmas red
234	□	762 Pale pearl gray
049	╱	3689 Light mauve
075	♡	3733 Medium dusty rose

BACKSTITCH

403	╱	310 Black–all stitches

Stitch count: 32 high x 28 wide

Finished design sizes:
25-count fabric –2½ x 2¼ inches
22-count fabric –2⅞ x 2⅝ inches
36-count fabric –1¾ x 1⅝ inches

CHRISTMAS STOCKING

Hang this stocking (shown on page 161) early to heighten the anticipation of Santa's arrival. Finished stocking is 18×12 inches.

MATERIALS
FABRICS
10×12-inch piece of 14-count white Aida cloth
¾ yard of blue velveteen
½ yard of fabric for lining
THREADS
Cotton embroidery floss in colors listed in the key on page 171
Gold metallic sewing thread
SUPPLIES
Needle; embroidery hoop
16×24-inch piece of fleece
3 yards of ⅛-inch-wide gold piping
6-inch piece of ⅛-inch-diameter gold cord for hanging loop
1 yard of 1½-inch-wide red satin ribbon
Two 1½-inch-high gold bells

INSTRUCTIONS
Tape or zigzag edges of Aida cloth to prevent fraying. Find the center of the chart and the center of the fabric. Begin stitching there.

Work cross-stitches using three plies of floss. Use two plies of DMC 103 and one ply of DMC 824 to work blended needle stitches. Use two plies to work the backstitches and French knots. Use one strand of the gold metallic thread for the straight stitches around star.

Enlarge the stocking pattern on page 169. Cut one front and back from velveteen and one front and back from lining fabric. Cut one stocking front from fleece.

Cut one 7×8½-inch piece of velveteen for cuff back. Cut two 7×8½-inch pieces from lining fabric for cuff.

Center Floba cloth on top of one piece of felt. Turn ¼ inch under on all edges and fuse the stitchery to the felt. Glue gold cord around edge of stitchery, butting ends together at the top.

Place second felt backing piece behind first felt piece. Stitch felt pieces together, attaching flat braid at the same time.

Tack two jingle bells and ribbon bow to the top of the ornament. Repeat instructions to make additional ornaments.

Place fleece on back of velveteen stocking front and machine-quilt in a 1-inch diagonal grid with gold metallic thread, if desired.

Trim stitched Aida cloth to 7×8½ inches. (This should leave ½ inch beyond stitching.)

Sew sides of velveteen cuff back to stitched Aida cloth cuff front, using ½-inch seam allowance. Stitch gold piping around top and bottom of cuff, ½ inch from raw edges.

Sew side seams of cuff lining front and back. With right sides together, stitch cuff lining to cuff top along lower edge.

Stitch gold piping around quilted stocking front, ½ inch from raw edge. (Do not stitch piping on top edge.) Sew the velveteen stocking back to front with right sides together, stitching on the piping stitching line; turn.

Make stocking lining by stitching lining back to lining front, leaving open at the top.

Insert stocking lining into velveteen stocking, wrong sides together. Turn ½-inch allowance at top edge to inside of stocking.

Insert raw edges at top of cuff between lining and stocking top. Insert gold cord for hanging loop on the right side of cuff at right side. Topstitch through all thicknesses around top of stocking to join the cuff to the stocking.

Turn cuff down. Tack red bow and bells in place.

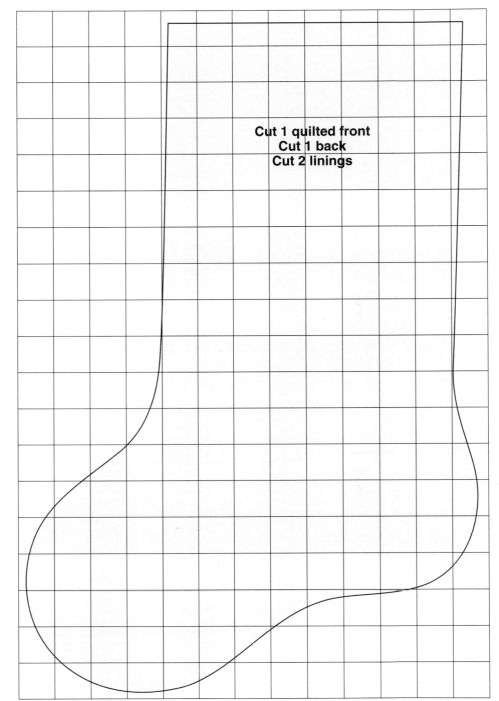

CHRISTMAS STOCKING PATTERN (½" seam allowance included)   **1 Square = 1 Inch**

Cut 1 quilted front
Cut 1 back
Cut 2 linings

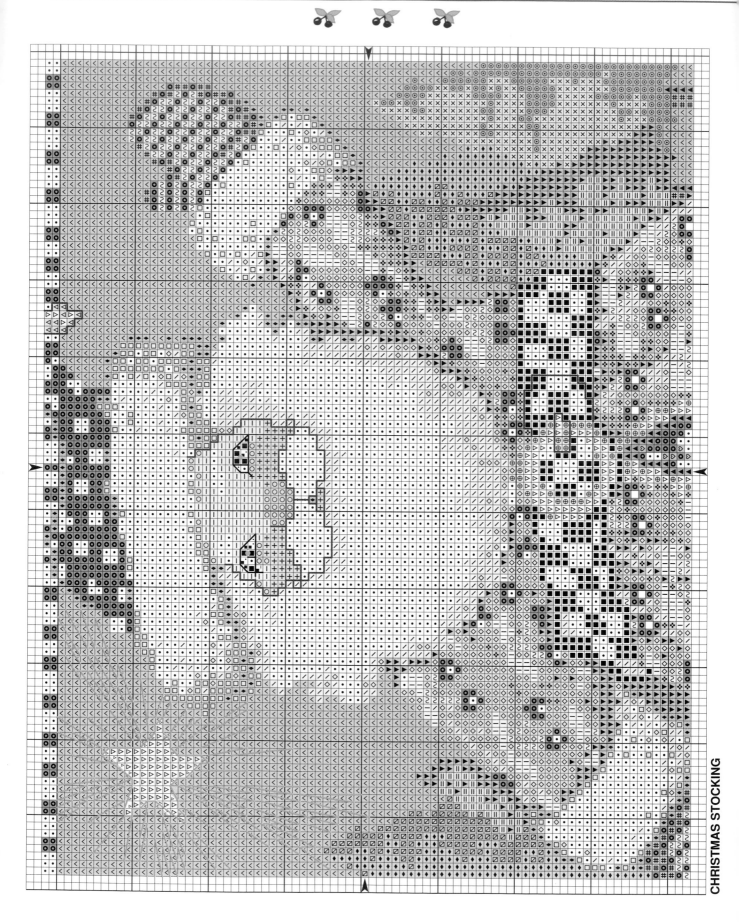

CHRISTMAS STOCKING

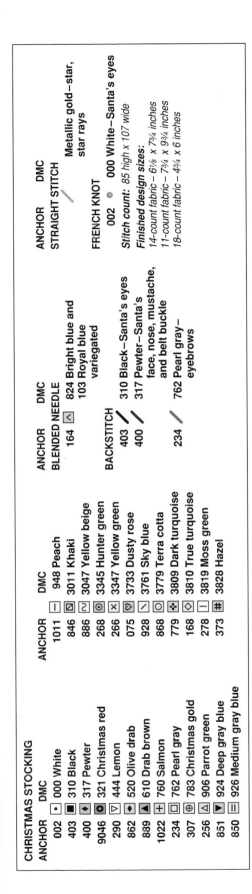

CHRISTMAS STOCKING

ANCHOR	DMC		ANCHOR	DMC	
002	·	000 White	1011			948 Peach
403	■	310 Black	846	⊠	3011 Khaki
400	◆	317 Pewter	886	∽	3047 Yellow beige
9046	⊙	321 Christmas red	268	⊙	3345 Hunter green
290	▽	444 Lemon	266	×	3347 Yellow green
862	◆	520 Olive drab	075	▷	3733 Dusty rose
889	◀	610 Drab brown	928	/	3761 Sky blue
1022	+	760 Salmon	868	○	3779 Terra cotta
234	□	762 Pearl gray	779	✣	3809 Dark turquoise
307	⊕	783 Christmas gold	168	◇	3810 True turquoise
256	◁	906 Parrot green	278	—	3819 Moss green
851	▶	924 Deep gray blue	373	⊞	3828 Hazel
850	⫿	926 Medium gray blue			

BLENDED NEEDLE

ANCHOR	DMC	
164	◁	824 Bright blue and 103 Royal blue variegated

BACKSTITCH

403	\	310 Black–Santa's eyes
400	\	317 Pewter–Santa's face, nose, mustache, and belt buckle
234	/	762 Pearl gray–eyebrows

STRAIGHT STITCH

ANCHOR	DMC	
		Metallic gold–star, star rays

FRENCH KNOT

002	●	000 White–Santa's eyes

Stitch count: 85 high x 107 wide
Finished design sizes:
14-count fabric – 6⅛ x 7¾ inches
11-count fabric – 7¾ x 9¾ inches
18-count fabric – 4¾ x 6 inches

Breit Ideas

This jolly holiday design will keep your stitching full of Christmas surprises.

Classic Mary Engelbreit cherries and checkerboards make wonderful motifs to embellish gifts. Think about a set of dinner napkins with the cherry motif in one corner. Checkerboard borders on place mats can be stitched in colors to match dinnerware. These quick-to-stitch motifs can decorate kitchen towels and hot pads.

Use Hoppy, Happy, and Harey, our fun-loving bunnies, to decorate wearables for kids of any age.

Isolate Santa from the background. One boot and a corner of his coat are the only places where you'll need to invent a few stitches. Trim your completed stitchery in a free-form shape and cut a matching piece for backing. Stuff with polyester fiberfill for a special doll or pillow. If you give your Santa to a youngster, substitute French knots for the seed beads.

The free-form star flowers on the border of this design are a creative springboard. Sprinkle them on cross-stitch bands to use on linens or wearables.

Use Santa's waving, mittened hand with the furry cuff to stitch tree ornaments and gift tags. Experiment with some angora yarn to stitch the cuff.

PEACE AND LOVE

ngels sing and lions purr a perfect melody. The joy of Christmas shines in this elegant Mary Engelbreit design where all the symbols of the season come together harmoniously.

*H*armony is the
message of this symbolic Christmas sampler,
opposite, *where the light of the star illuminates a*
lion and lamb, and a joyful chorus reaches out to
the reindeer and Christmas trees in the border.

Reindeer fly on this bow, above, embellishing
a basket of holly. Make the bow for a Christmas
wreath or to decorate a gift with a
personal touch.

175

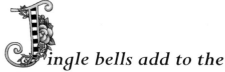

*J*ingle bells add to the
merriment illustrated by your cross-stitches. This festive pillow,
above, *deserves a place of prominence in your holiday home.*

Elements from the Peace and Love design create joyous season's
greetings. Stitch the banner of harmony with its musical theme on
a greeting card, opposite left, *and embellish a serving tray,*
opposite right, *with a singing angel.*

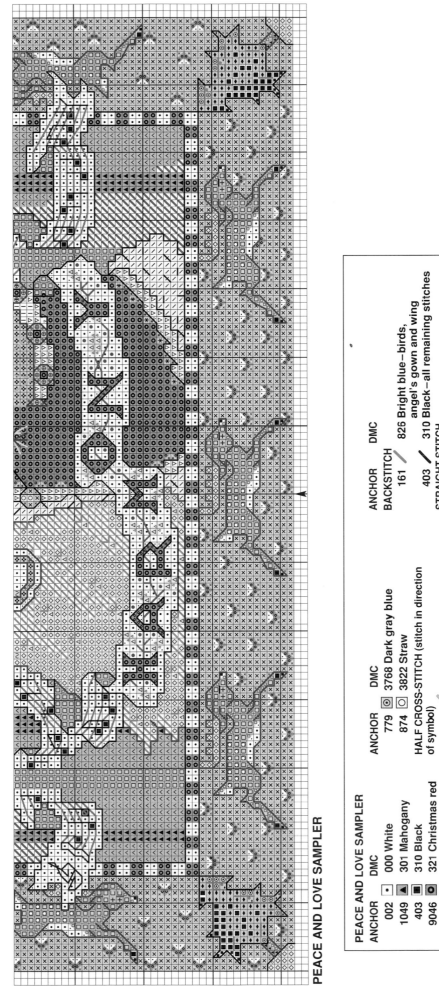

PEACE AND LOVE SAMPLER

PEACE AND LOVE SAMPLER

ANCHOR		DMC
002	·	000 White
1049	◀	301 Mahogany
403	■	310 Black
9046	◉	321 Christmas red
398	⟲	415 Pearl gray
362	□	437 Tan
290	▷	444 Medium lemon
266	◁	471 Avocado
303	⊕	742 Tangerine
307	✕	783 Christmas gold
043	◪	815 Garnet
023	⟋	818 Pink
134	⟨	820 Royal blue
161	✦	826 Bright blue
158	◇	828 Powder blue
052	+	899 Rose
851	◆	924 Deep gray blue
1010	—	951 Ivory
246	✳	986 Forest green
886	⟋	3047 Yellow beige
292	▬	3078 Pale lemon

ANCHOR		DMC
779	⊙	3768 Dark gray blue
874	○	3822 Straw

HALF CROSS-STITCH (stitch in direction of symbol)

266	╱	471 Avocado–angel's wing (2X)
134	╱	820 Royal blue–background (2X)
158	╱	828 Powder blue–angel's gown (2X)

BACKSTITCH

002	╱	000 White–lion's claws, halo, border trees, lamb's collar
1049	╱	301 Mahogany–hair, harp, deer, border trees, face, hands, drum
9046	╱	321 Christmas red–birds, horn
290	╱	444 Medium lemon–bird beaks and feet
134	╱	820 Royal blue–lamb's sweater, star, angel's gown

ANCHOR		DMC
BACKSTITCH		
161	╱	826 Bright blue–birds, angel's gown and wing
403	╱	310 Black–all remaining stitches

STRAIGHT STITCH

1049	╱	301 Mahogany–mane
403	╱	310 Black–drumsticks (4X)
290	╱	444 Medium lemon–tassel
851	╱	924 Deep gray blue–banner
779	╱	3768 Dark gray blue–musical staff
	╱	Kreinik Japan #5 gold thread–harp (1X), drum (2X)

FRENCH KNOT

002	○	000 White–deer, drum cord
403	●	310 Black–birds' eyes
9046	●	321 Christmas red–berries

Stitch count: 135 high x 140 wide

Finished design sizes:
11-count fabric – 12¼ x 12¾ inches
14-count fabric – 9¾ x 10 inches
18-count fabric – 7½ x 7¾ inches

PEACE AND LOVE SAMPLER

All the symbols of joy are found in this one harmonious holiday design (shown on page 174).
Finished design is 12¼×12¾ inches.

MATERIALS

FABRIC
18×18-inch piece of 11-count white Aida cloth

THREADS
Cotton embroidery floss in colors listed in the key on page 179
Four additional skeins of DMC 783
One additional skein of DMC 321 and white
Gold metallic thread

SUPPLIES
Needle; embroidery hoop
Frame and mat of choice

INSTRUCTIONS

Tape or zigzag edges of Aida cloth to prevent fraying. Find the center of the chart and the center of the fabric. Begin stitching there.

Work cross-stitches using three plies of floss. Use two plies of floss for the half cross-stitches. Use two plies of floss to work the backstitches, straight stitches, and French knots. Use one strand of the gold metallic thread for the angel's lyre and two strands for the drum.

Frame and mat as desired.

CHRISTMAS BOW

Reindeer on a cross-stitch band brighten a bow on a basket (shown on page 175) or a wreath.
Finished bow is 12 inches wide.

MATERIALS

FABRIC
26-inch length of 22-count 3¼-inch-wide Christmas green cross-stitch band

THREADS
Cotton embroidery floss in colors listed in the key below right

SUPPLIES
Needle
5 yards of 1½-inch-wide picot-edged ribbon
Three 1-inch-diameter red jingle bells
18-inch piece of cotton-covered floral wire

INSTRUCTIONS

Find the center of the chart and the center of the cross-stitch band. Begin stitching there.

Work cross-stitches using three plies of floss over two threads of the cross-stitch band. Use two plies of floss to work the backstitches and French knots. Repeat stitching the design to desired length.

Sew the ends of the cross-stitch band together to form a circle.

Cut two 26-inch pieces of picot-edged ribbon and sew the ends together, making two circles.

Fold the cross-stitch band in half with the seam at center back. Fold each ribbon circle in half with seam at center back. Slip ribbon inside cross-stitch band.

String three jingle bells on wire and wrap wire around center of cross-stitch band and ribbon, gathering to form a bow.

Make another bow from picot-edged ribbon, leaving ends of ribbon extended. Wire the first bow with cross-stitch band on top of second bow.

Use ends of wire to attach bow to a basket or wreath.

CHRISTMAS BOW		
ANCHOR	DMC	
002	⊡	000 White
403	■	310 Black
9046	◉	321 Christmas red
362	▢	437 Tan
023	⊘	818 Pink
158	⊗	828 Powder blue
BACKSTITCH		
403	╱	310 Black–all backstitches
FRENCH KNOT		
002	○	000 White–deer

Stitch count: 18 high x 76 wide
Finished design sizes:
22-count fabric – 1¾ x 7 inches
28-count fabric – 1⅜ x 5½ inches
36-count fabric – 1 x 4¼ inches

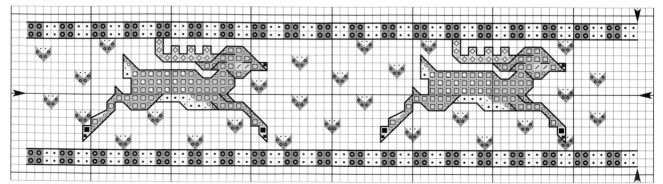

CHRISTMAS BOW

GREETING CARD

GREETING CARD

Harmony is a message of friendship. The note you send with this stitched musical motif is appropriate for Christmas or anytime (shown on page 177). Finished card is 5×7 inches.

MATERIALS

FABRIC
8×8-inch piece of 14-count oatmeal Aida Plus

THREADS
Cotton embroidery floss in colors listed in the key at right

SUPPLIES
Needle
10×7-inch piece of art paper
Tracing paper
Crafts knife
1 yard of metallic gold baby rickrack
3 gold musical charms
Crafts glue

INSTRUCTIONS

Find the center of the chart and the center of the Aida Plus. Begin stitching there.

Work cross-stitches using three plies of floss. Use two plies of floss for the backstitches, straight stitches, and French knots.

Fold art paper in half to make a 5×7-inch card, trim lower edge with pinking scissors, if desired.

Trace oval pattern provided below. Draw oval on back side of card front, centering it ¾ inch below the fold and 2 inches above the bottom edge. Carefully cut out oval using a crafts knife.

Glue two rows of gold rickrack around opening. Attach charms with needle and floss.

Trim Aida Plus to 3¾×7 inches with design centered. Place stitchery behind oval and glue or tape in place.

GREETING CARD

ANCHOR		DMC	
002	·	000	White
403	■	310	Black
9046	◉	321	Christmas red
290	▽	444	Medium lemon
266	△	471	Avocado
023	∕	818	Pink
158	◇	828	Powder blue
052	+	899	Rose
292	I	3078	Pale lemon

BACKSTITCH

9046	∕	321	Christmas red–birds
290	∕	444	Medium lemon–birds
161	∕	826	Bright blue–birds
403	∕	310	Black–all remaining backstitches

STRAIGHT STITCH

| 779 | ∕ | 3768 | Dark gray blue–banner, musical staff |

FRENCH KNOT

| 403 | ● | 310 | Black–birds' eyes |
| 9046 | ● | 321 | Christmas red–berries |

Stitch count: 23 high x 77 wide
Finished design sizes:
14-count fabric – 1⅝ x 5½ inches
11-count fabric – 2⅛ x 7 inches
18-count fabric – 1¼ x 4¼ inches

**GREETING CARD
PATTERN**

CHRISTMAS PILLOW

CHRISTMAS PILLOW		
ANCHOR	DMC	
002 ·	000	White
1049 ▲	301	Mahogany
403 ■	310	Black
9046 ⊙	321	Christmas red
398 ∼	415	Pearl gray
362 □	437	Tan
290 ▽	444	Medium lemon
266 △	471	Avocado
303 ⊕	742	Tangerine
307 ✕	783	Christmas gold
043 ♥	815	Garnet
023 ╱	818	Pink
161 ✦	826	Bright blue
158 ◇	828	Powder blue
052 +	899	Rose
851 ◆	924	Deep gray blue
1010 −	951	Ivory
246 ✳	986	Forest green
886 ◲	3047	Yellow beige
292 ⊡	3078	Pale lemon

ANCHOR	DMC	
779 ◉	3768	Dark gray blue
874 ◯	3822	Straw

HALF CROSS-STITCH (stitch in direction of symbol)

002 ╱	000	White—angel's gown
398 ╱	415	Pearl gray—angel's gown and wings
290 ╱	444	Medium lemon—harp
266 ╱	471	Avocado—angel's gown
303 ╱	742	Tangerine—harp
161 ╱	826	Bright blue—angel's gown
158 ╱	828	Powder blue—angel's gown

BLENDED HALF CROSS-STITCH (stitch in direction of symbol)

002 ╱	000	White and
266	471	Avocado—angel's wing
002 ╱	000	White and
158	828	Powder blue—angel's gown

BACKSTITCH

002 ╱	000	White—lion's claws, halo
1049 ╱	301	Mahogany—hair, harp, faces

ANCHOR	DMC	
BACKSTITCH		
134 ╱	820	Royal blue—angel's gown
161 ╱	826	Bright blue—angel's gown and wing
403 ╱	310	Black—all remaining stitches
STRAIGHT STITCH		
1049 ╱	301	Mahogany—mane, tassel
290 ╱	444	Medium lemon—tassel
851 ╱	924	Deep gray blue—banner
779 ╱	3768	Dark gray blue—musical staff
		Kreinik gold #8 braid—harp, drum, drumsticks
FRENCH KNOT		
9046 ●	321	Christmas red—berries

Stitch count: 94 high x 94 wide

Finished design sizes:
14-count fabric – 6¾ x 6¾ inches
11-count fabric – 8½ x 8½ inches
18-count fabric – 5¼ x 5¼ inches

CHRISTMAS PILLOW

The rhythm of the holidays is captured in this salute to the sounds of Christmas (shown on page 176).
Finished pillow is 8×13¾ inches, not including ruffle.

MATERIALS
FABRICS
12×12-inch piece of 14-count white Aida cloth
9×9-inch piece of red velveteen
1 yard of green moiré taffeta
⅓ yard of white cotton fabric
THREADS
Cotton embroidery floss in colors listed in the key on page 182
Gold metallic braid
SUPPLIES
Needle; embroidery hoop
⅔ yard of 1¾-inch-wide flat gold braid
9×14½-inch piece of fleece
1⅓ yards of ⅛-inch-diameter gold piping
Ten ½-inch-diameter gold jingle bells
Polyester fiberfill

INSTRUCTIONS
Tape or zigzag edges of Aida cloth to prevent fraying. Find the center of the chart and the center of the fabric. Begin stitching there.

Work cross-stitches and half cross-stitches using three plies of floss. Use two plies of floss to work the backstitches, straight stitches, and French knots. Use one strand of metallic braid to work the straight stitches.

Trim Aida cloth to 9×7¾ inches with design centered.

Cut velveteen in half to make two 9×4½-inch pieces. To make pillow top, stitch velveteen pieces to each side of cross-stitched Aida cloth, using ½-inch seams.

Sew flat gold braid to velveteen on each side of the stitchery. Place fleece behind pillow top and baste in place around outer edges.

Sew gold piping around pillow top, ½ inch from edges.

Cut a 9×14¾-inch piece of taffeta for pillow back. Cut 6-inch bias strips from taffeta, piecing as necessary to make an 88-inch length. Join ends, using ½-inch seam, to make a circle.

Fold taffeta circle lengthwise with wrong sides together. Press along fold. Sew a gathering thread through both layers of ruffle, ½ inch from raw edges. Pull threads to fit perimeter of pillow front with raw edges even; adjust gathers evenly. Sew ruffle to pillow along piping stitching line.

Sew pillow front to back, right sides facing, keeping ruffle tucked inside. Leave an opening for turning. Clip the corners and turn right side out.

Sew 5 gold jingle bells evenly spaced on top of gold braid on each side of the stitchery.

Make a pillow form by stitching two 9×14¾ pieces of white cotton fabric together, leaving an opening for turning and stuffing. Turn and fill with polyester fiberfill; whipstitch the opening closed.

Insert pillow form inside pillow; whipstitch the opening closed.

ANGEL TRAY

Holiday entertaining becomes even more festive when an angel on a tray helps you serve guests (shown on page 177).
Finished tray is 9½×9½ inches.

MATERIALS
FABRIC
14×14-inch piece of 28-count white Jubilee cloth
THREADS
Cotton embroidery floss in colors listed in the key on page 185
SUPPLIES
Needle; embroidery hoop
9½×9½-inch red serving tray
10×10-inch piece of fleece
Crafts glue
1¼ yards of ¼-inch-wide red and gold braid

INSTRUCTIONS
Tape or zigzag edges of Jubilee cloth to prevent fraying. Find the center of the chart and the center of the fabric. Begin stitching there.

Work cross-stitches and half cross-stitches over two threads of Jubilee cloth using three plies of floss. Use two plies of floss to work the backstitches and French knots. Use one strand of gold metallic braid for straight stitches.

Trim the finished stitchery to 10×10 inches with design centered. Cover cardboard insert supplied with tray with fleece, turn ½ inch of fleece to back of cardboard, and glue in place.

Center stitchery over fleece-covered insert, turn edges to back, and glue in place.

Glue braid around front edges of insert. Assemble tray following manufacturer's instructions.

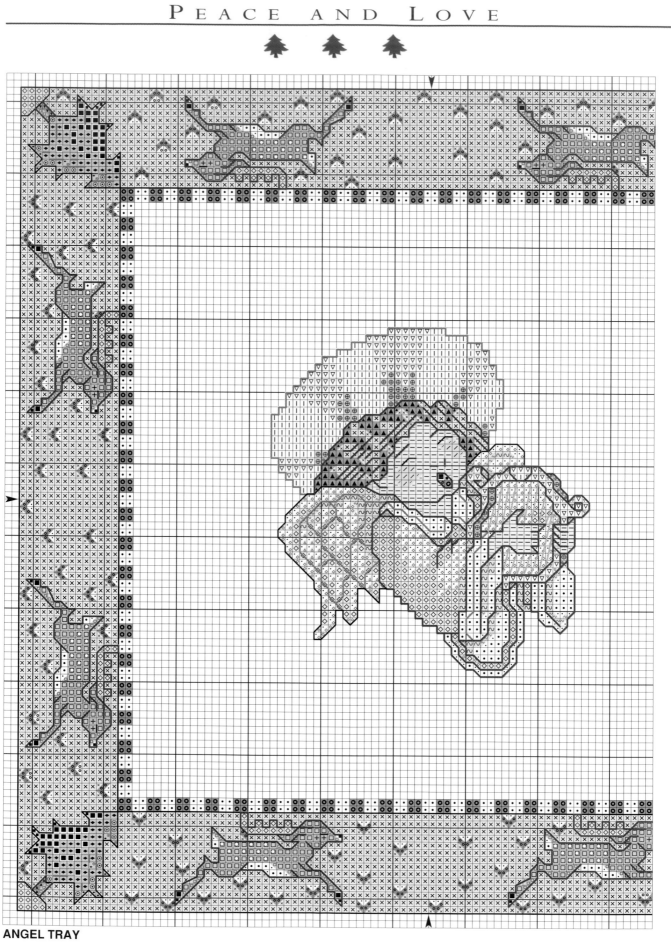

ANGEL TRAY

Breit Ideas

Your love of stitching will be fulfilled by this Peace and Love design's year-long applications.

🌲 Busy little birds line up across the top of this sampler. Stitch these chipper songbirds on a cross-stitch band for linens or wearables. Dot a toddler's apparel with cross-stitched birds or perch them on top of one another for a bookmark.

🌲 Make a music book cover using the banner from the Greeting Card chart. Follow the general instructions for making an album cover on page 87.

🌲 Christmas place settings are just a few stitches away. Stitch one reindeer on a cross-stitch band for a napkin ring. (Just whip the ends together and the napkin ring is finished.) Use the tree from the border corners for a corner of a napkin. Stitch one or a whole row of flying reindeer on a place mat.

🌲 Kids love drums, so stitch a drum logo on a toddler's shirt.

🌲 Trim your tree with angels stitched on Aida Plus or perforated paper and backed with felt for a joyful decoration. Add sparkle by substituting beads for floss on the halo.

🌲 Shrink the Christmas bow by stitching just two reindeer on a narrower piece of cross-stitch band. Glue a reindeer stitched on perforated paper to a card for a gift tag.

ANGEL TRAY

ANCHOR		DMC	
002	·	000	White
1049	▲	301	Mahogany
403	■	310	Black
9046	◎	321	Christmas red
398	~	415	Pearl gray
362	□	437	Tan
290	▽	444	Medium lemon
266	△	471	Avocado
303	⊕	742	Tangerine
307	×	783	Christmas gold
023	⁄	818	Pink
158	◇	828	Powder blue
052	+	899	Rose
851	◆	924	Deep gray blue
1010	−	951	Ivory
292	I	3078	Pale lemon
779	◉	3768	Dark gray blue

ANCHOR		DMC	
BACKSTITCH			
002	⁄	000	White—border trees, halo
1049	⁄	301	Mahogany— hair, harp, deer, border trees, face, hands
403	⁄	310	Black—border trees, eyes
134	⁄	820	Royal blue—angel's gown
161	⁄	826	Bright blue—angel's gown and wing
STRAIGHT STITCH			
	⁄		Kreinik gold #8 braid—harp
FRENCH KNOT			
002	○	000	White—deer

Stitch count: 114 high x 114 wide

Finished design sizes:
28-count fabric – 8¼ x 8¼ inches
22-count fabric – 10⅜ x 10⅜ inches
36-count fabric – 6⅓ x 6⅓ inches

CROSS-STITCH BASICS

GETTING STARTED
Cut the floss into 15- to 18-inch lengths and separate all six plies. Recombine the plies as indicated in the project instructions and thread into a blunt-tipped needle. Rely on project instructions to find out where to begin stitching.

BASIC CROSS–STITCH
Make one cross-stitch for each symbol on the chart. For horizontal rows, stitch the first diagonal of each stitch in the row. Work back across the row, completing each stitch. On most linen and even-weave fabrics, stitches are usually worked over two threads as shown in the diagrams, *below*. Each stitch fills one square on Aida cloth.

Cross-stitches also can be worked in the reverse direction; just remember to embroider the stitches uniformly. That is, always work the top half of the stitch in the same direction.

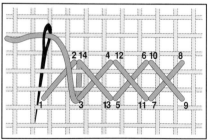

Basic Cross-Stitch in Rows

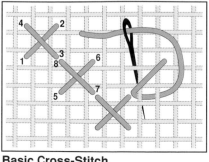

**Basic Cross-Stitch
Worked Individually**

HOW TO SECURE THREAD AT BEGINNING
The most common way to secure the beginning tail of thread is to hold it under the first four or five stitches.

Or, you can use a waste knot. Thread needle and knot end of thread. Insert needle from right side of fabric, about 4 inches away from placement of first stitch. Bring needle up through fabric and work first series of stitches. When stitching is finished, turn piece to right side and clip the knot. Rethread needle with excess floss and push needle through to the wrong side of stitchery.

When you work with two, four, or six plies of floss, use a loop knot. Cut half as many plies of thread, but make each one twice as long. Recombine plies, fold the strand in half, and thread all the ends into the needle. Work the first diagonal of the first stitch, then slip the needle through the loop formed by folding the thread.

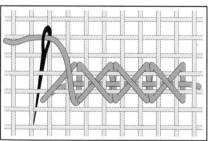

How to Secure Thread at Beginning

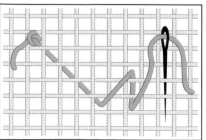

Waste Knot

HOW TO SECURE THREAD AT END
To finish, slip threaded needle under previously stitched threads on wrong side of fabric for four or five stitches, weaving thread back and forth a few times. Clip thread.

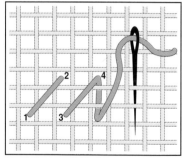

How to Secure Thread at End

HALF STITCHES
A half cross-stitch is simply a single diagonal or half of a cross-stitch. Half cross-stitches usually are listed under a separate heading in the color key and are indicated on the chart by a diagonal colored line in the desired direction.

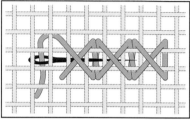

Half Cross-Stitch

QUARTER AND THREE–QUARTER STITCHES
Quarter and three-quarter cross-stitches are used to obtain rounded shapes in a design. On linen and even-weave fabrics, a quarter stitch extends from the corner to the center intersection of threads. To make quarter stitches on Aida cloth, you'll have to estimate the center of the square. Three-quarter

FABRIC/NEEDLE/FLOSS		
FABRIC	TAPESTRY NEEDLE SIZE	NUMBER OF PLIES
11-COUNT	24	THREE
14-COUNT	24–26	TWO OR THREE
18-COUNT	26	TWO
22-COUNT	26	ONE

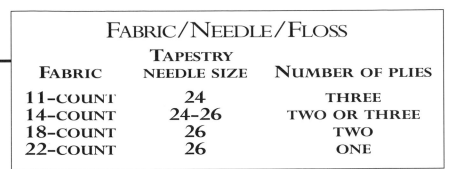

stitches combine a quarter stitch with a half cross-stitch. Both of these stitches may slant in any direction.

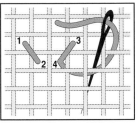

Quarter Cross-Stitch

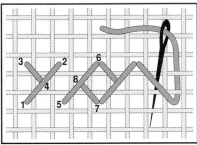

Three-Quarter Cross-Stitch

CROSS-STITCHES WITH BEADS

When beads are attached using a cross-stitch, work half cross-stitches, and attach beads on the return stitch.

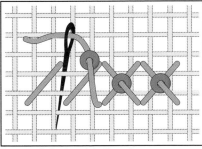

Cross-Stitch with Bead

BACKSTITCHES

Backstitches are added to define and outline the shapes in a design. For most cross-stitch projects, backstitches require only one ply of floss. On the color key, (2X) indicates two plies of floss, (3X) indicates three plies, etc.

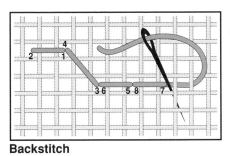

Backstitch

FRENCH KNOTS

Bring threaded needle through fabric and wrap floss around the needle as illustrated. Tighten the twists and insert needle back through the same place in the fabric. The floss will slide through the wrapped thread to make the knot.

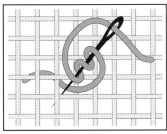

French Knot

WHIPSTITCHES

A whipstitch is an overcast stitch that often is used to finish edges on projects that use perforated plastic. The stitches are pulled tightly for a neatly finished edge. Whipstitches also can be used to join two fabrics together.

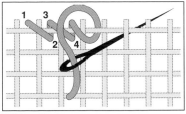

Whipstitch

FEATHERSTITCHES

This decorative stitch produces a featherlike shape as long or as short as desired. Bring threaded needle to front at top of feather. Insert needle back into fabric approximately four threads away, leaving stitch loose. Bring needle to front again, slightly lower than center of first stitch; catch thread from first stitch. Repeat in an alternating motion until desired length is achieved. End feather by stitching a straight-stitched quill.

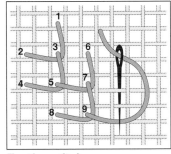

Featherstitch

LAZY DAISY STITCHES

To make this petal-shaped stitch, bring the needle to the front. Using a sewing-style stitch, insert the needle back through the same hole and out again two or more threads away, catching the loop under the needle. Gently pull to shape the loop. Push the needle back through the fabric on the other side of the loop to tack the loop in place.

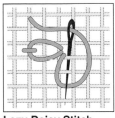

Lazy Daisy Stitch

CROSS-STITCH BASICS

MATERIAL FOR CROSS-STITCH

Counted cross-stitch has become a popular form of stitchery. Many stitchers like to work cross-stitch designs on different fabrics and use different threads than are specified in the projects. The following information will help you understand the projects in this book so you can adapt them to your own needs.

CROSS-STITCH FABRICS

Counted cross-stitch can be worked on any fabric that will enable you to make consistently sized, even stitches.

Aida cloth is the most popular of all cross-stitch fabrics. Threads are woven in groups separated by tiny spaces. This creates a pattern of squares across the surface of fabric and enables a beginning stitcher to easily identify where cross-stitches should be placed. Aida cloth is measured by squares per inch; 14-count Aida cloth has 14 squares per inch.

Aida cloth comes in many varieties. 100-percent cotton Aida cloth is available in thread counts 6, 8, 11, 14, 16, and 18. 14-count cotton Aida cloth is available in more than 60 colors. For beginners, white Aida cloth is available with a removable grid of prebasted threads.

Linen is considered to be the standard of excellence for experienced stitchers. The threads used to weave linen vary in thickness, giving linen fabrics a slightly irregular surface. When you purchase linen, remember that the thread count is measured by threads per inch, but most designs are worked over two threads, so 28-count linen will yield 14 stitches per inch. Linens are made in counts from 14 (seven stitches per inch) to 40.

Even-weave fabric also is worked over two threads. The popularity of cross-stitch has created a market for specialty fabrics for counted cross-stitch. They are referred to as even-weave fabrics because they are woven from threads with a consistent diameter, even though some of these fabrics are woven to create a homespun look. Most even-weave fabrics are counted like linen, by threads per inch, and worked over two threads.

Hardanger fabric can be used for very fine counted cross-stitch. The traditional fabric for the Norwegian embroidery of the same name has an over-two, under-two weave that produces 22 small squares per inch.

Needlepoint canvas is frequently used for cross-stitching, especially on clothing and other fabrics that are not suitable alone. Waste canvas is designed to unravel when dampened. It ranges in count from 6½ to 20 stitches per inch. Cross-stitches also can be worked directly on mono-needlepoint canvas. This is available in colors, and when the background is left unstitched, it can create an interesting effect.

Sweaters and other knits often are worked in duplicate stitch from cross-stitch charts. Knit stitches are not square; they are wider than they are tall. A duplicate-stitched design will appear broader and shorter than the chart.

Gingham or other simple plaid fabrics can be used, but gingham "squares" are not perfectly square, so a stitched design will seem slightly taller and narrower than the chart.

Burlap fabric can easily be counted and stitched over as you would a traditional counted-thread fabric.

THREADS FOR STITCHING

Most types of thread available for embroidery can be used for counted cross-stitch projects.

Six-ply cotton embroidery floss is available in the widest range of colors, including variegated ones. Six-ply floss is made to be separated easily into single or multiple plies for stitching. Instructions with each project in this book tell you how many plies to use. A greater number of plies will result in an embroidered piece that is rich or heavy; few plies will create a lightweight or fragile texture.

Rayon or silk floss is similar in weight to cotton floss, but the stitches have a greater sheen. Either thread can be exchanged with cotton floss, one ply for one ply, but because they have a "slicker" texture, they are slightly more difficult to use.

Pearl cotton is available in four sizes: #3, #5, #8, and #12 (#3 is thick; #12 is thin). It has an obvious twist and a high sheen.

Flower thread is a 100-percent cotton, matte-finish thread. A single strand of flower thread can be substituted for two plies of cotton floss.

Overdyed threads are being introduced on the market every

day. Most of them have an irregularly variegated, one-of-a-kind appearance. Cotton floss, silk floss, flower thread, and pearl cotton weight threads are available in this form. All of them produce a soft shaded appearance without changing thread colors.

Specialty threads can add a distinctive look to cross-stitch. They range in weight from hair-fine blending filament, usually used with floss, to $\frac{1}{8}$-inch-wide ribbon. They include numerous metallic threads, richly colored and textured threads, and fun-to-stitch, glow-in-the-dark threads.

Wool yarn, usually used for needlepoint or crewel embroidery, can be used for cross-stitch. Use one or two plies of three-ply Persian yarn. Select even-weave fabrics with fewer threads per inch when working cross-stitches in wool yarn.

Ribbon in silk, rayon, and polyester becomes an interesting texture for cross-stitching, especially in combination with flower-shaped stitches. Look for straight-grain and bias-cut ribbons in solid and variegated colors and in widths from $\frac{1}{16}$ to $1\frac{1}{2}$ inches.

TYPES OF NEEDLES

Blunt-pointed needles are best for working on most cross-stitch fabrics because they slide through holes and between threads without splitting or snagging the fibers. A large-eyed needle accommodates the bulk of embroidery threads. Many companies sell such needles labeled "cross-stitch," but they are identical to tapestry needles,

blunt-tipped and large-eyed. The chart on page 187 will guide you to the right size needle for most common fabrics. One exception to the blunt-tipped needle rule is waste canvas; use sharp embroidery needles to poke through that fabric.

Working with seed beads requires a very fine needle to slide through the holes. A #8 quilting needle, which is short with a tiny eye, and a long beading needle with its longer eye are readily available. Some shops carry short beading needles with a long eye.

CROSS-STITCH TIPS

PREPARING FABRIC

The edges of cross-stitch fabric take a lot of abrasion while a project is being stitched. There are many ways to keep fabric from fraying while you stitch.

The easiest and most widely available method is to bind the edges with masking tape. Because tape leaves a residue that's almost impossible to remove, it should be trimmed away after stitching is completed. All projects in this book that include tape in the instructions were planned with a large margin around the stitched fabric so the tape can be trimmed away.

There are some projects where you should avoid using masking tape. If a project does not allow for ample margins to trim away the tape, use one of these techniques: If you have a sewing machine readily available, zigzag stitching, serging, and narrow hemming are all neat and effective methods. Hand-

overcasting also works well, but it is more time consuming.

Garments, table linens, towels, and other projects that will be washed on a regular basis when they are finished should be washed before stitching to avoid shrinkage later. Wash the fabric in the same manner you will wash the finished project.

PREPARING FLOSS

Most cotton embroidery floss is colorfast and won't fade. A few bright colors, notably reds and greens, contain excess dye that could bleed onto fabrics if dampened. To remove the excess dye before stitching, gently slip off paper bands from floss and rinse each color in cool water until the water rinses clear. Then place floss on white paper towels to dry. If there is any color on the towels when the floss is dried, repeat the process. When completely dry, slip the paper bands back on the floss.

CENTERING THE DESIGN

Most of the projects in this book instruct you to begin stitching at the center of the chart and fabric. To find the center of the chart, follow the horizontal and vertical arrows on the chart to the point where they intersect.

To find the center of the fabric you're using, fold the fabric in half horizontally, and baste along the fold. Then fold the fabric in half vertically, and baste along the fold. The point where the basting intersects is the center of the fabric. Some stitchers like to add some additional lines of basting every 10 or 20 rows as a stitching guide.

Breit Finishes

Show off those hours of cross-stitching by putting some extra thought into the finishing of your projects.

CLEANING YOUR WORK

You may want to wash your needlecraft pieces before mounting and framing them because the natural oils from your hands eventually will discolor the stitchery. Wash your piece by hand in cool water using mild detergent. Rinse several times, until the water is clear.

Do not wring or squeeze the needlecraft piece to get the water out. Hold the piece over the sink until dripping slows, then place flat on a clean terry-cloth towel, and roll tightly. Unroll the stitchery and lay flat to dry.

PRESSING YOUR WORK

Using a warm iron, carefully press the fabric from the back before framing or finishing it. If the piece has lots of surface texture stitches, place it on a terry-cloth towel or other padded surface to press.

FRAMING YOUR DESIGN

Use determines how cross-stitch pieces should be mounted and framed. Needlework shops, professional framers, and craft stores offer many options.

For most purposes, omit the glass when framing your cross-stitch. Moisture can build up between the glass and the stitchery, and sunlight is intensified by the glass. Both can cause damage to the fabric. If you must use glass, be sure to mat the piece so the stitchery does not touch the glass.

• Keep your finishing options open by stitching on a large piece of fabric. The specified fabrics in this book provide approximately 3 inches of excess fabric on all sides of the design.

• No matter how you finish your stitchery, keep it straight. Even-weave fabric is easy to line up against a mat or another fabric. Likewise, it is easy to see when it isn't perfectly straight. Double or triple mats provide added emphasis for your stitchery. When taking your completed stitchery to a frame shop, be sure to select a framer with needlework experience.

• Color selection of mats, frames, and other finishing materials should come from the stitchery. Select colors from your cross-stitches that you want to accent, making sure they complement the stitchery rather than overpower it.

• Pad it. Stitchery is meant to be soft. One or two layers of fleece behind your stitchery makes all the difference in framed pieces as well as pillows, banners, frames, and inserts. Even when a smooth look is desired, it is important to back your stitchery with a piece of lightweight fabric (batiste or muslin) to achieve that smoothness.

• When sewing is a part of the finishing, transparent nylon thread will keep your stitches invisible. On projects where sewing is difficult, use tacky fabric glue. A professional finish for bookmarks, ornaments, picture frames, and many other cross-stitched products is achieved with just a little dab of fabric glue.

• Add extra texture. Charms, buttons, tassels, ribbon bows, or pom-poms can add that finishing touch. Pay attention to color matching. Try making your own tassels using embroidery floss selected from the color key of your stitchery.

• Combine your stitchery with unexpected fabrics that capture the mood of your piece. Suede, chamois, moiré taffeta, and felt are used as well as cotton fabrics to accent the cross-stitches in this book. Match the weight of the fabric to your completed stitchery. If you find that the perfect fabric to accent your cross-stitches is of lighter weight, use an interfacing to bring it to comparable weight.

• Cording and flat braid trims are a beautiful secret to success. They not only provide a finishing touch, but they also can hide a corner that isn't as smooth as you'd like.

• Have a place for your stitchery in mind. Consider the room and the specific area where you want to display your cross-stitches as you select finishing materials.

• Remember, your cross-stitches are what you want to see when you finish. Extra attention and embellishment can showcase your work with style and prestige.

INDEX/SOURCES

INDEX of PROJECTS

INDEX of SAYINGS

INDEX of PHOTOGRAPHS

Scott Little: Pages 3, 4–5, 8–9, 10, 11, 12, 13, 25, 26, 36–37, 38, 39, 40, 50–51, 52, 53, 54, 66, 68, 96, 97, 110–111, 112, 113, 114, 115, 142–143, 144, 145, 146, 147

Wm. Hopkins, Hopkins Associates: Pages 22–23, 24, 27, 41, 55, 64–65, 67, 69, 78–79, 80, 81, 82, 83, 92–93, 94, 95, 126–127, 128, 129, 130, 131, 156–157, 158, 159, 160, 161, 170–171, 172, 173, 174, 175

Barbara Elliott Martin: Pages 6–7

SOURCES

• Cross-stitch fabrics for the entire book are from Zweigart Fabrics/Joan Toggitt Ltd., 2 Riverview Dr., Somerset, NJ 08873.

• The finished wood pieces used with cross-stitch inserts are all from Sudberry House, Old Lyme, CT 06371. These include the small hand mirror, page 46; the Shaker pincushion box, page 59; the small collector's cabinet, page 120; the oak rectangular box, page 125; the faux box, page 141; and the small square tray, page 183.

• The paperweight, page 151, is from Yarn Tree Designs, P.O. Box 724, Ames, IA 50010.

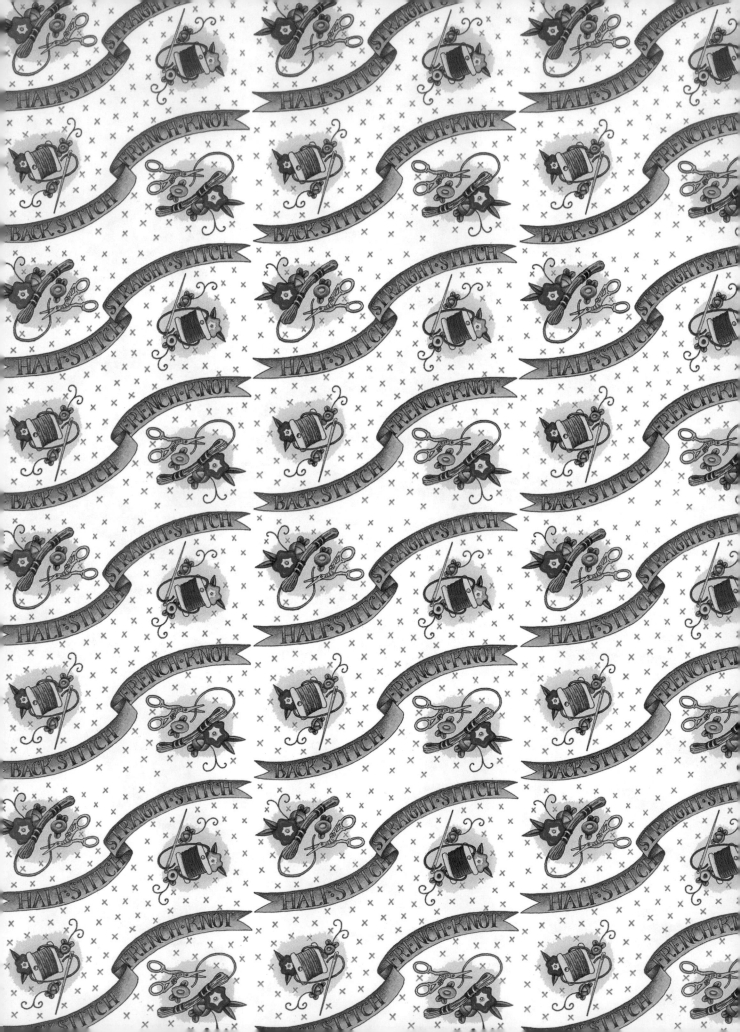